Never Summer
A Thousand Rainbows

Stan Nicholas

A Buff and Beyond Ink—Longmont, CO
ISBN: 9798218030919
eBook ISBN: 978-1-0878-5218-8
Library of Congress Control Number: 2022912323
Title: *Never Summer: A Thousand Rainbows*
Author: Stan Nicholas
Digital distribution | 2022
Paperback | 2022

Dedication

This book is dedicated to my parents who started their family during the Great Depression and closely followed and understood the rules of survival, learning to make meager ends meet without any thought of government subsidy. I would love to have had the wisdom of reflection during those early years to fully appreciate what they were both willing to do to protect and provide for their family, and for the legacy of faith that has threaded its way through four generations.

Inside Cover Picture

As you ease into my story this photo gives you a glimpse of where and how we lived for many nights of the 13 summers of the book's story. The photo shows the family mode of transportation and me and my three sisters hanging our heads out of the entrance to our mobile motel.

Prologue

It may or may not be coincidental that my story unfolds a year and one half into a new administration attempting to find its way through the morass of culture change that has plagued our great nation since 9/11. One issue front and center is the phenomena of immigration, and our attempt to deal with the complications of immigrants, both legal and illegal and how they fit in with our culture, economy, and entitlement programs once designed only for our citizens. We claim that they are welcome here because most will perform the menial jobs that Americans simply refuse to do.

For 13 years my family experienced the culture of being migrant laborers and living a life that many of the millions of immigrants are encountering today. I have thought many times as I witness their stories and their plight through the various media sources, about what has changed over the years of my life that would find a white, Anglo Saxon family with educated parents facing the trials of migrant fruit pickers, populated today solely with the ranks of immigrants, mostly from south of our border.

Certainly, anthropology played its part in those 13 extraordinary years of my life. I was greatly impressed and influenced by the book, _The Glass Castle_ by Jeanette Walls because of a number of similarities in her life and in mine. The parental issues of her life were different from those of my parents, who were both very responsible people. The common thread of her early life and mine was the roamer style of existence that I experienced in the summer months of my formative years. Like Jeanette and her siblings, I and my siblings all became moderately successful people with careers, families, nice homes with well-educated kids. My memories of those years recalls that my family never received one scintilla of assistance from our welfare systems—no food stamps, no living subsidies, no welfare checks or free health care. My siblings and I funded our college educations without student loans.

With the inclusion of our summer income from fruit tramping and my father's job as a teacher, my family lived on no more than seven to eight thousand dollars a year while purchasing a home and owning one automobile. I know for certain that ten percent of that amount was given to our church, my father being an obedient tither. On our never-miss Sundays throughout the summer I clearly remember my dad putting cash in the collection plates of the churches we visited. So, on the meager amount remaining after gifting and the IRS, we still managed to thrive. I recall never thinking that I was a kid from a poor family but clearly still recognized the class structure within the small community of Denison, Iowa, where I was born and nurtured.

What did sink in through the simple process of osmosis and absorption and without hearing a constant reminder from parents or peers was that the many challenges that life presents are the very building blocks to having a purpose driven life and finding success not defined by wealth and possessions. But, more so characterized by faith, meaningful relationships, and hope, and caring for those less fortunate than ourselves. Having now observed the vagaries of my generation and the two plus since, it is clear how radically things have changed. I could write a whole book about the glaring contrasts from then and now as it relates to defining what constitutes a successful life, but allude to those distinctions in chapters throughout the book, without going beyond my sociological wavelength by suggesting to be a know all or cure all for humanity's afflictions.

On a recent trip to my paternal roots in the U.K., mostly Ireland and Scotland, my wife, Suzi and I met a couple who had a number of life experiences and challenges that were similar to ours. On one particular Guinness-infused discussion, the other gentleman and I concluded that many of the world's problems could be solved by four mandatory requirements of the world's, mostly US, children: All must serve either in the military or Peace Corp type of commitment following high school, no cell phone possession until age 18, compulsory labor-for-allowance, and join 4-H. Simple minded but dazzling.

Chapter One

"…you listen, you teach me, mama/
And, I know inside you care/So get down,
down here beside me/Ooh, you ain't
going nowhere."
Phil Collins
Genisis

I remember the day clearly, although it has been some 20 years since I moved my mother into a care facility. It was gut wrenching to watch this 82-year-old matriarch, mother of four enter so unwillingly into her new home. Like so many people in this stage of life, I am convinced it usually triggers the beginning of the end for them, at first mentally followed by physical decline.

In the short period of one day when this unfortunate life event happened, I found myself thinking about the extraordinary life of this woman and the uncommon sacrifices that most mothers in this era would never have faced in the course of their life journey.

She was born in 1909, lived in a home without running water or electricity. She was one of nine children of immigrant German parents, who helped her family eke out a living by working on their farm and only managed to finish high school.

She married a schoolteacher in northern Iowa in the late 20's, had four children and was a stay-home mom for most of her children's secondary school lives.

As I helped her move into the assisted living facility, I couldn't help being in awe of what she endured in her life and due to a bizarre set of circumstances, became a mother to a migrant labor family, cooking meals on a Coleman stove, living in harvest shacks and often times making home in a '49 Chevy while traveling between Iowa and fruit harvest venues in the northwestern United States.

I vaguely remember courses in anthropology that helped us understand the various cultures throughout the world's history and how the circumstances of geography, sociology, economics, and other factors shape the course of those lives. Such is the case of this story.

One of the worst times in a person's life if we are lucky enough to outlive our parents, and when circumstances force us into such decisions, is that day when we remove a parent or parents from their home of many years and place them in a 'care' facility. Those decisions are often prompted by a default mentality adopted by modern western civilizations.

As their children, we claim to be too busy to have them live with us, or that we both work, so placing them in our home would be no different than them living alone in their own home. Or, we convince ourselves that they have become a danger to themselves and thus, can no longer live alone safely. Oftentimes, there are legitimate medical reasons for the move, but too often the decision to move them to a care facility is one of convenience and expedience.

My father died far too prematurely at the age of 61 of heart disease. My mother, in spite of a difficult and challenging life, lived for another 30 years as a widow, mostly alone, until her move into a care facility, suffering with dementia for most of her last 10 years of life.

I managed her physical, financial, and medical needs from the day of my father's estate probate hearing. I went in to visit her almost every day for the 10 year period that she resided away from her home. She often wanted me to take her for a home visit which I did many times. We had kept and maintained her home, although unoccupied, for the duration of her life. It was always a repeated, sad exit to return her to Fraser Meadows.

In the waning years of her life, the level of confusion accelerated and she often questioned who I was and why I was in her room. Sometimes she was totally dialed in and knew I was me. I went in one day for a visit and the nurse who was her primary caregiver suggested that I gather the family, which seemed like an ominous suggestion. I asked her why she was advocating the gathering of family, and she stated that my mother had quit eating her favorite food, desserts. She said that when people in their advanced years choose to quit eating, it is their way of selecting the exit ramp from life. Three days following, I got the call that she had passed.

So many years hence, I think that the late-in-life decisions by children have changed somewhat in that the affluence of people today allows those decisions to be more hastily made and at much earlier stages of life. There are also different entry level assisted living structures to entice those decisions, now allowing elderly people to move to a nice place with little or no assistance and gradually move along as care needs increase. A perfect world would follow the practice of cultures such as Native Americans or Asians, keeping two or more generations together so that the flow of care giving, wisdom sharing and preparation for each family member's onset of aging as a learning tool and not an albatross.

Never Summer portrays an unusual set of circumstances that mold the lives of its players, who if they had been raised in almost any other environment, likely would never have experienced the unique and captivating path through life. As you will read, my mother and father were warriors and fierce champions for their family. They were tough, full of grace, hardworking and fearless in many adversarial settings throughout our summer jaunts.

Chapter Two

T here are a myriad of dynamics that shape a person's life, from the unique human genome that fashions one's personality, to their life's vision and aspirations that carve a road to the future. When I think back on my formative years, I realize that I was undeniably molded by the influences on my life from a small number of people: teachers, bosses, friends and teammates, coaches and siblings, parents, and of course, the indelible DNA fomented within my embryo. Equally influential in my sculpting was the milieu of my birthplace, the origin and setting for my particular American dream, and the opening act for my adolescent years. I lived the first 18 years of life on North 16th street in Denison, Iowa, just two blocks south of the municipal water tower so prevalent on the landscapes of small, rural communities throughout the fruited plains, the archaic, four-legged sentinel proclaiming in large bold letters and tinsel town graphics the title of a famous movie from the 50's, *"It's A Wonderful Life."* The movie featured Jimmy Stewart and the older sister of one of my high-school flames and fellow thespian, Donna Reed. If you are reading this and

you know these actors, this book is for you. If you don't recognize their names due to being 'born too late,' then this book is for you also.

I've bragged many times during my life of that fact—winning a 'most outstanding actor' award, costarring with Donna's sister, Karen Mullenger, my co-lead in *Lavender and Old Lace*, our senior class play. We had never dated each other because she was an attraction to the upperclassmen and she was above my pay grade for a possible mate. We were both sophomores at the time, but ended up as dates at her invitation to the Spring Prom. I had a few dalliances prior to that night with another girl or two and some experimental kissing. After the event I drove her home with my brand new driver's license and our new (used) 58 Chevy Bel Air.

She lived on a farm near town and the lane to her home was resplendent with freshly planted corn fields with luxuriant sprouts erupting from their furrows incessantly marching skyward striving to reach the zenith of their survival, the sun and the rain. The lane was long and sandwiched by enormous deciduous trees, hedgerows, and the fields and very secluded from the entry point and the house. I had little clue as to what such a hideaway offered and had little inclination to find any reason to stop there for a while.

I was new at driving and found or sought no correlation between being alone in a car with a girl friend and one of a small few opportunities to find privacy.

Nonetheless, I did stop, probably to give us a chance to talk while alone with little forethought for much beyond that. I really had no rational thought about her Senior boy friend nor had any serious attachments to a girl at that point in my life. There was a term, 'necking,' that I had a sophomoric, simple understanding of without the help of a Webster. Somehow, we ended up necking. It was a little discomforting because for me it was classic on-the-job training and I didn't want my naivete to be apparent. I was surprised at how aerobic, breathing as though I had just competed in a sprint track event. All I could think about was what her boyfriend, David Johnson, would be thinking.

She was his invitee to the prom, but a prior sledding accident earlier in the year had broken both of his femurs and he was unable to attend. She had the option to select a substitute, and likely because of our friendship, trust, and sharing school activities in student government, forensics, plays, and competition with me in spelling bees. We were almost always the last two standing and gloated when we triumphed over the other.

Davy, two years our senior and more advanced in the things that young boys learned in locker rooms and school bus rides had sort of paved the way for the things I was just getting into the classroom for. I did like the training and Karen was the perfect scholar–she was beautiful, had Jolie lips, let me go at my newbie pace and provided a wokeness that may have taken me a few years to figure out on my own. Every young lad at some point in life figures those things out, and that was my launch.

Adolescents today are faced with a staggering number of stunning entrance ramps and enormous pressure to expedite the pace, beyond what once was considered normal. I am thankful for the way it all began; completely innocent, mysterious and romantic, electrifying and glorious for a wet-behind-the-ears 16 year old neophyte that kept me in my comfort zone and chaste.

The social mores in the 50's were defined by the pastors of local churches, and parishes, the lyrics of songs from Pat Boone, Patsy Cline, Rosemary Clooney, and from the screenplays of movies that had no rating system because the script wasn't filled with cuss bombs and trashy scenes. TV was defined by The Little Rascals, Westerns, Howdy Doody, and Ed Sullivan–a far cry from the plethora of X and R rated flix, the sickness of twirp dancing, rap lyrics that would embarrass anyone over 40. I have always hoped that caskets are void of sound systems for hearing our songs.

When I look through old high school yearbooks at Karen and eventual new flames, I believe that the mystique and discovery of one's early years were truly enhanced by the innocence and curiosity of a young chap's mind which makes reminiscing all the more sweet and romantic.

I have since lived through the generation of my three daughters and currently in the observation mode of the current generation in which all of my grandchildren now inhabit. It should be obvious to all that the moral compass of sexuality has changed. (I can't actually use the word evolved as that would suggest positive progression).

During my three daughter's middle and high school years I was the committee chairperson for a local Young Life chapter. I remember a study that was done at that time that compared the top 10 issues of character development and behavioral traits that challenged people such as teachers, coaches, and parents. In my era, it was passing notes in class, throwing spitballs, belching, cussing with words like dam, shit, dumbass, stupid, etc. Dropping out of school topped that list. On a rare occasion a young high school girl would suddenly disappear only to find out that she had gone to live with an aunt for a while. In my Young Life years in the 70's and early 80's the lowest infraction on the list was smoking on the school property, followed by alcohol abuse and occasional joint smoking, topped by a new phenomenon of threatening suicide. During that time I learned that my girl's high school had a class called Teen Parenting. When I inquired with a Young Life acquaintance who led that class about its purpose, she stated that it was for high school girls and a few boys who had become parents prematurely. When I asked how big the class was, she stated that it was currently 46 in number.

During that time I was also actively involved with the school board and joined a group of parents and fiercely fought an effort to add abstinence education to the curriculum. We lost that battle. Forty years hence, I need not paint the picture of the changes that plague the youth of today. In those 70's times we had 'praying at the pole' (flag) to begin the school day, and Young Life was allowed space on the school campus and had a vibrant ministry to many troubled high school kids. Certainly I am not suggesting that allowing God in some form to roam the halls of public education would cure some of the ills, but my guess is that it would positively affect some. A good friend, once the principal at our girl's high school for a number of years, abruptly resigned after he had disciplined some young students at a Friday night football game. Five or so boys from the school arrived at the game fairly inebriated and he would not allow them entrance. Instead, he suggested that he call a cab to take them home as they were obviously impaired. The following Monday morning several of the parents came in unannounced and as a group, became belligerent, complaining that they felt it was wrong for the principal to act as judge of their son's blood alcohol level and then take on the role of judge and jury. Soon after, our school lost the best, in my opinion, principal it ever had. He had also been the high school boys' basketball coach and led them to the only basketball state championship in the school's history.

Chapter Three

Denison, Iowa, probably differed very little from the thousands of similar sized farming communities of the Midwest. They flourished after the depression and as farms became productive, the nearby towns prospered by giving support to the commerce created by agriculture and by catering to and supplying the occupants of the farms. Entrepreneurs followed and opened businesses to service the populace of the small communities. Denison had its array of stores and shops and service-minded businesses.

There was a plethora of churches of all denominations, a couple of movie theaters, a bowling alley and a skating rink where I first fell in love on a Saturday in May, roller skating with my middle-school sweetheart, Diana Lyman to the "do-not-forsake-me" droning of Frankie Lane's "High Noon," a 50's recording hit. Our musical tastes are indelibly and mysteriously molded by the peculiar librettos and harmonies of our era's music once etched into the vinyl spherical grooves of 45's and 33 1/3 rpms that were stacked like flapjacks on shelves and coffee tables, but are now incarcerated by the thousands in match book sized electronic MP3 Carnegie Halls, that so soon also became obsolete with the addition of Siri and Alexa music and information platforms that bring every song known to man and the encyclopedia Britannica into your kitchen.

My Junior High years saw the initiation of boy-girl hand holding and other inventive ways of coming into contact with the opposite sex, providing blissful opportunities in our otherwise puritanical lives. Roller skating, basement dance parties and meetings at movie theaters were about the sum total of the venues that could provide a haven for those early social interactions. I think I was twelve years old when I first kissed a girl. It was passionately shared with Diana during a neighborhood party for classmates and friends in her parent's basement. The Saturday morning roller skating 'couple skate' was the precursor of that blessed and opening act when a few weeks later during the party we industriously found a small space beneath the steps that led from the upper floor to the party room. I recall that a few of our friends were generating their own hormonal activation, but I paid little heed to what they were doing so that I could pursue my own infatuations.

Even though Denison was probably just like many other similar-sized cities, my perception was that it was uniquely different and better than any of the other towns with which I was familiar, especially the towns that Denison competed with in sports and other school events. I think the Beach Boys were thinking of small-town America when they wrote and crooned, "Be True to Your School." I always thought that the people from those other towns were really weird, wore funny clothing and were nowhere near our level of sophistication and competence in just about everything. I didn't even think their cheerleaders were attractive when most any young lad in high school would normally think that all cheerleaders were dazzling, had model-like legs demurely adorned with bobby socks, and could vie for homecoming queen even though they all did pretty much the same inane cheers, leg kicks and pom shakes.

Denison, however small and bourgeoisie, had a very defined class society, much like India, but without the multi-layered class strata so defined by India's caste system. India's social structure was onerously displayed in the latter decades of the century by Mother Theresa's mission that ministered to the 'untouchables' of that country's culture. Denison nonetheless was comprised of a very distinct upper and lower class with a sprinkling of farmers and service-minded people mixed in between the two obvious core groups. Civilizations throughout the history of the world have always had classes of people who perceived that they were superior and expectant of subservience from the not-so-blessed, and Denison, Iowa, was the poster child of small-town American cities.

My home on North 16th street, although some four blocks north of the main drag of the town and geographically distanced from the lower, Boyer river end of town and the railroad tracks, was still 'across the tracks,' not so much from its location, but more a result of who we were as a family, how my father was employed, where we worshiped, our income level and our status in the community relative to our non-membership in the right civic organizations, and the country club.

My father, who had come from a middle class family, whose father, my grandfather, a failed bank owner during the depression years, had to drop out of medical school after completing his undergrad years and first year of medical school due to the financial disaster of the Great Depression. He had completed a degree in Education prior to medical school and was forced by financial constraints to go into teaching and to give up on his dream of becoming an osteopathic physician.

He ended up teaching and coaching basketball in Everly, Iowa, a very small town in Eastern Iowa before moving our family to Denison in the late 30s, accepting a teaching position at Denison High School where he taught math, industrial arts and vocational prep.

I survived the archaic birthing process in late October of 1942 as did my mother, who was administered anesthesia at the behest of our family doctor, Dr. Grau, by my father placing ether laced gauze over my mother's mouth until she was somewhat comatose. Dr. Grau was preoccupied with the considerable obstetrical concerns on how to deliver a baby with the substantial cranial girth that seemed to predominate the gene pool of my siblings and me.

I followed my two older sisters, four and two years my seniors into rural Iowa life, a few years' shy of being a baby boomer. I could easily have been a product of the boom of babies that resulted from post-war frolics in the hay intimately reuniting military vets and their wives. However, my father had been unable to serve due to having severely flat feet, making my earthly unveiling a few years shy of the war's end.

One additional female sibling four years later not only prompted a tube-tying intervention in the family fecundity, but also a move to a newer, bigger home on North 16th where I would live the balance of my pre-college years.

With the advent of a much more diverse cultural dimension in many cities of the US, my observation is that some changes have happened, but the bullying that was minimal in the 50's has taken on a frightful dimension to the disenfranchised legions of ethnic, faith following and physically contrasting kids in whatever form that might be.

Chapter Four

"There's no one quite like Grandma
And I know you will agree
That she always is a friend to you
And she's a friend to me."
St Winifred's School Choir

As I have mentioned, North 16th street was distant from the railroad tracks of our town, but was part of a neighborhood so much like a majority of the hoods in Denison. The lower end neighborhoods predominated and were scattered throughout the hilly geography that contoured western Iowa. But, there were a few enclaves where the privileged adorned the city with their upscale homes and classy cars. They thought of themselves as the gentry in our little town. I'm not sure how or what determined the membership of the various classes of those mid-century Midwestern urban factions, but I suspect that one's position in any given culture is somewhat predetermined by occupation and income level, much as it is today.

My family's social circles were defined pretty much by church affiliation and neighborhood friendships. The county club at the edge of town had a small golf course and a clubhouse that I was never privileged to set foot in until my 20th high school reunion. As architectural changes along with the country's development, the older buildings could have won contests for retro art deco examples from that era. Or, as a display in one of the tacky museums that exhibited the architecture of previous epochs. The clubhouse was much smaller than I had remembered and was somewhat shabby by contemporary standards but was still the functional meeting place for members of the country club. Looking around the place during my time at the reunion suggested that either the country club membership had fallen on hard times by the 80's and no longer enjoyed the status of the earlier decades, or the perceptions of grandeur and importance that I had placed upon that group was unrealistic and overblown.

My very earliest memories of life in our home probably happened when I was about four years old. I vividly remember playing with a couple of neighborhood friends, Phyliss Frahm, her brother Phil and one or two others, a boy and a girl whose names I can't recall. It was a warm summer day and we were in the shade of our concrete-walled garage that protruded from a hill, the top of which was at ground level and an extension of our house. It was a hot day and we all were dressed in shorts and bare chested. Phyliss was my age, so her bared chest wasn't noticeably different or of much interest, but for some reason known only to four-year olds, the gathered little rascals on that day, the interest in exploring each other's anatomy became the day's highlight and then, too quickly the antonym.

I became pretty surprised to discover that the girls were so much differently plumbed than I and was getting pretty intrigued by that reality when the exploration came to an abrupt end with the appearance of my mother. She put a quick end to our little science project. It was a very early lesson in how things that are so sensual and risque are likely to be morally out of bounds.

Throughout the rest of my years in Denison, Phyliss and Phil continued to be close neighborhood friends without any further dalliances among us. It may have been poetic justice that some years later, Frahm's dog, an Irish Setter, jumped up and bit me in the face, fileting my adolescent nose that today still bears a noticeable scar.

At a somewhat recent high school reunion for both the classes of 1960 and 1961, both of the Frahms were in attendance. In the social time before dinner, Phil, whom I hadn't seen since high school came over to say hello. He proceeded to thank me for saving his life, literally. We were probably 12 and 11 respectively and had gone swimming at an edge-of-town gravel pit before the Memorial Day opening of our town pool. Phil had attempted to swim out to a floating dock, discovering about halfway there that he couldn't make it to the dock or back to the shore. I jumped in and somehow managed to drag him back to shore, both of us coughing and choking together. I had pretty much forgotten the incident until that evening.

Our next-door neighbor to the north was a lady whose first name I either never knew or had forgotten. Most of the kids who lived near our home called her Grandma Frahm. She was the true grandmother of Phyllis and Phil but no less of a grandmotherly caregiver to many of the young people who lived nearby. She was famous for making a summertime drink that, to this day, I don't recall that I have ever tasted since, egg lemonade. She also made great homemade bread and cinnamon rolls on an old wood-burning oven/stove that she fueled with corncobs, so plentiful from the fields that she once farmed. I spent many hours with my friends and siblings in Grandma Frahm's kitchen drinking her famous drink and eating her pastries.

Perhaps because I had been virtually without grandparents, I thought that Grandma Frahm was my own grandmother. I didn't learn the truth of that until my own grandfather, Wilhelm Fischer, my mother's father, came to live with us when I was nine. When trying to appraise the connection between Grandpa Fischer and Grandma Frahm I finally discovered that the latter was a grand mom only in spirit and grace. I learned the associated reality that there are people who, because of their generosity and love, are capable of showing adoration and affection beyond the bond of family. I honestly think that my old neighborly Grandma Frahm was as much a grandmother to me and my sisters as she was to her own grandchildren, who lived a block further away.

Grandma Frahm's declining years gave me my first glimpse of the infirmities that we now identify as dementia, and Alzheimer's, but was referred to then as 'going crazy.' Regardless of how we named it then or refer to it now, it was my first dose of the profound sadness of seeing the afflictions that beset people that had so abundantly earned our love and respect.

Chapter Five

"Up in the morning and off to school
The teacher is teaching the Golden Rule,
American History and practical math
working hard you're hopin' to pass."
Chuck berry
School Days

I have very few memories of my earliest years which psychologists claim is normal for most people. There are a few recollections that come to mind in my early school years, the first being somewhat unpleasant. I clearly recall my first day of kindergarten and all the usual hype that is dumped on first-day students who are usually emotionally overwhelmed with apprehensions about the experience about to unfold.

I didn't believe that I was going to like it as much as I was promised. My mother may have walked with me to school, some four blocks from home, or I had been dropped off by my father who was a teacher at the nearby high school. The teacher, Mrs. Welch, rang an old-fashioned hand bell and stated that she wanted each person to find a partner and to hold hands with them and line up to enter the building. Kay Boeck, who was destined to become one of the early leaders of radical feminism, aggressively did as she had been told, sought me out, grabbed my hand and we proceeded two by two into the old, school building.

I wasn't about to have anything to do with that plan, broke free of my bondage and headed for home. On my short journey back home I encountered Mr. Whitehead, the milk delivery man about a block from school, who asked me why I wasn't in school. I responded that I had the day off, which I think set an early tone for my attitude about cultural and scholastic entrapments for the rest of my life. Upon arriving home, my mother quickly reorganized my thinking, promptly returning me to school just in time for me to roll out a small rug along with my classmates, lie down and take a nap. That welcomed activity got me properly adjusted and I went on to a less than enthusiastic induction to elementary education.

My other vivid school memory was two years later, when I immediately fell in love with my second-grade teacher, Ms. Richel. She was a babe, very kind and I perceived that she liked me far better than any of my schoolmates. It's strange how a good relationship with a teacher can have such an impact on a student's comprehension and success in the classroom.

Some of my fondest and most distant memories were of seasonal events in the early years of my life. My dad and my mom were born in 1909 on May 12 and 13, respectively, separated by just one day at birth and in death by almost 30 years. As I mentioned, my father died young and quickly of heart disease and my mother lived as a widow for three more decades.

They were born in northern Iowa near the town of Lake Park. They had the good foresight and fortune to buy a small two-room cabin that they had moved to a small lot on Lake Okoboji, a prime tourist attraction that was acclaimed by <u>National Geographic</u> as one of the five bluest lakes in the world and one of the most beautiful. We spent many of my early childhood weekend days at the Lazy Lagoon neighborhood and languished away the hours playing by our boat dock catching turtles and small sunfish and lazing around in the warm sun.

One of my father's favorite possessions that were severely limited in number by his teacher's salary was the purchase of an Alumnacraft fishing boat that we rowed around the confines of the off-lake lagoon. My dad owned a small three-horsepower motor that slowly buzzed us around from place to place and got us to where we found some great fishing for perch, bass, and crappies. When my father died in the early 70's, neither my mother nor my siblings had any interest in maintaining a long-distance maintenance of the cabin after our move to the west, so we sold it for a song, only to later regret that decision as Okoboji property became one of the most sought resort properties in the entire Midwest. Looking back on the event of selling our cabin property is a great example of one of those big life lessons that I mentioned in the first paragraph—that hindsight optics are always much clearer than future and present revelation.

I had quite a number of relatives living in northern Iowa, and southern Minnesota. My mother had 7 siblings and my father, two. All of the aunts, uncles and cousins lived within a 10-mile radius of Lake Park and all on my mother's side were farmers.

My favorite relative of all was my dad's sister, aunt Mary. She was indescribably wonderful in so many ways. I could probably author an entire book on the unusual characteristics of so many of my kin, but the story would likely mirror the stories of most midwestern farm families. What can't be left out of this story is the most interesting thing for which aunt Mary was famous. As far as I can recall, she had no medical training in her earlier life, but she had remedies for most of the common afflictions of that era. She was convinced that most of the disorders could be cured by having an enema, and that most of those same maladies would never have happened had we adhered to her conviction that routine enemas would cure all. Trips to northern Iowa to visit were likely the healthiest of all jaunts that we made, because none of us would admit to having the slightest gastrol disorders fearing the dreaded anal intrusion. How would that look and work in today's woke culture? But, I can assure you it was done in the spirit of promoting good health.

Another major event in my early years was to ride with my dad to the city dump of Denison after dark and do some target practice with a treasured possession, a 1909, .22 caliber Marlin slide action pump rifle. When I was just old enough to be trusted with a firearm I was taught how to carefully use a firearm by an older man who was a friend of my fathers who asked him after church one Sunday if I owned a rifle. When my father confirmed that I did not, he told us that he was having an estate sale and might have just the perfect rifle for me to learn to shoot. Prior to that I had become a deadly marksman with a Daisy Red Ryder BB gun having plinked thousands of bbs at tin cans, spatzies (our chosen name for sparrows) and an occasional alley garage window. I thought the word spatzie had been created and invented by my friends and I, only to discover later in life that it was a universal vernacular term used by young boys throughout the fruited plains and localized spellings and pronunciations demonstrated the variances of geographic and cultural differences. A later-in-life friend insisted that the Pennsylvania version of the name was actually, sputzie. And another friend from my Army days who was from the hills of Arkansas argued that sparrows were properly called spotzies. Names notwithstanding, they were the unfortunate prey of many childhood marksmen.

I persistently prodded my father to go look at the gun until he finally relented and took me to the sale. When I saw the rifle, I was possessed to possess it, but I fully expected to get the 'we'll see' response that would likely forever delay the purchase and allow someone else to buy it. We were very poor and my dad's oft repeated 'we'll see' retorts to other fixations of his children was always prompted by his inability to afford most of the things that we lusted for. I think that my dad knew that I was about to wet myself over the rifle so he asked the old gentleman how much he wanted for it. He responded that $2 dollars was the price. My dad knew that he was just being patronizing and gracious and told him that he couldn't in good conscience pay so little for such a treasure. The old gentleman said that if I didn't purchase it that he would give it to Goodwill or whichever recycling organization existed in that place and time and so I quickly forked over my own $2 and bought this magnum opus that I own and enjoy to this day. As I reflect on this event, I am sure that this relatively wealthy man as evidenced by the magnitude of his estate sale knew that a young man who otherwise could not afford such a firearm would help make his day and mine by staging the whole scenario. It is episodes like this and the noteworthy personages in the scenes and chapters of life that mold and sculpt the composition of who we become.

On warm nights I would plead with my dad to take me to the dump for some target practice. The uninformed might rightfully ask how one would consider a trip to a city dump at night conducive to shooting a rifle as a good venue for plinking. I would save up my paper route money to buy ammo and when

I had enough for two boxes, 100 rounds, I would start cajoling my chauffeur to pick a night to go. First of all, shooting during the day was problematic in that families like mine who hauled their own trash would be likely unwarranted targets as would the commercial trash haulers. Most important was the fact that my targets only came out at night, the ubiquitous legions of rats that took up residence at city dumps and other grimy places. I would sit on the right front fender of my dad's car so that he could still see enough to drive in the dark. We would turn off the headlights when we got close, drive up to the piles of garbage looming as large hills in the darkness and then my dad would stop, turn on the high beams and those large hills would literally swarm with rats that would freeze their gaze at the light beams and would become my adversary. We would stay until all of the rounds became empty cartridges, adding a lot of brass to the garbage piles along with at least 100 dead rats. I always made a war game out of the events of the evening and likely would have won the Medal of Honor if the results of my rampage had been enemy soldiers. I was either an accomplished assassin sniper or there were so many rats with little space between their bodies that I just couldn't miss.

I could go on about some of my favorite childhood escapades, but I really don't remember many more because there weren't many more. Most young men growing up in the 40's and 50's lived their big adventures during the summer months when scout outings, fishing trips, forts and tree houses helped form and later spin the tales of the early years that defined their boyhood recollections.

It was following my second grade school year that my life and my summertime odysseys were about to take on a whole new set of latitudes and languishes that would clearly define my self-esteem, my educational endeavors and my gone-forever leisurely boyhood summers and the cheeks of tan.

Chapter Six

"Back in 1948, we took our old V8
And when it had gone a hundred thou
We got out and pushed it a while."
John Denver
On the Road

My mom was essentially a stay-at-home mother and my dad managed, almost, to keep us all fed, clothed and under a dry roof in spite of his meager income as a schoolteacher. We always had supplemental income projects to help make ends meet. For many years, my siblings and I would go door-to-door selling pure, strained honey that we would buy from Otto Versluce, an old German farmer who was a beekeeper and a friend of my parents.

We would carry our quart and gallon containers in a red American Flyer coaster wagon through the streets of Denison without qualm. I don't remember who kept the proceeds of our endeavor, but I do remember that we developed more than adequate sales skills, or we were the recipients of the compassionate response of our neighbors and customers feeling sorry for our sorry little asses.

Another of our entrepreneurial pursuits was to head to the Iowa cornfields sometime in the fall to glean popcorn that had been missed by the corn harvest machines. We would bring multiple bushels home and tediously put them through a hand driven corn sheller one ear at a time. Weeks of labor would produce several hundred pounds of the world's best popcorn (sorry, Nebraska) that we would once again canvas the neighborhood to sell. I am now a University of Colorado Buffalo sports fan and still have a horrible taste for Nebraska corn or the Huskers.

Sometime during my second grade year my father had a friend in the teaching profession who had taken his family on summer-long jaunts to the northwestern US on fruit picking vacations the previous two summer seasons. I would find out soon enough that the word, vacation, was a serious misnomer and that our excursions into seeking supplemental income would take on a whole new meaning of the *summertime blues* immortalized in the lyrics of a Del Shannon song of the same name.

My father was so infatuated by his friend's stories and emboldened by his claims of financial success that he couldn't resist a chance for adventure and fortune. Prior to that next summer, I can't recall ever going any further from our home than Lake Okoboji, some 100 miles north of Denison, for a family outing. At seven years of age I couldn't possibly have appreciated the extent of planning that took place in the months prior to our departure, the very day following the end of the school year, to the cherry orchards of the West.

We should have suspected that all would not become peaches and cream when my dad was able to contact and successfully get harvesting jobs at the very same orchard where the other family had toiled the previous two summers, and incidentally, wasn't going back for a third year. That would not likely have deterred my father from his plans, especially after his elaborate preparation and his new invention.

Using his skills honed from teaching industrial arts, shop and his woodworking genius, my father likely created one of America's very first RV, built to fit on the roof of our 1949 two-door, six cylinder Chevrolet. It had a very distinctive appearance, looking much like a very mini version of an aircraft carrier on wheels. The

sides of this car-top sleeper extended far beyond the width of the car and was supported by suction cups vacuuming tightly to the roof with two vertical posts at its posterior corners that extended down and attached to the bumper, giving it support where it extended beyond and over the sloping rear end of that model of Chevy.

When the end of our travel day brought nightfall, we would either find a campground, a city park, or a deserted side road to set up shop. At campsites in some of the most desolate parts of the earth I often heard my father say that if we lived here we'd be home now. It may have been humorous the first time that he said it, but soon became one of those inane things that parents repeat far too many times and were never again funny, but still cherished parts of our memories and expressions, and that we would eventually inflict on our own children in similar surroundings many years hence. Other such limericks will be forthcoming in later chapters where appropriate.

Our car top sleeper would become our home away from home for the five or six nights that it would take to travel between Iowa and Oregon and when we would travel from one harvest venue to the next. When we were ready to settle in for the night, we would hopefully find a level spot, set the emergency brake, and prepare our home. It was designed so that cradle-like sidebars would extend from the sides to give added width to the sleeping area. The front and rear tent shaped ends would then fold up on hinged joints that would lock in place to create a tent-like enclosure that was about six feet wide by 12 feet long.

We would enter from the rear end on an aluminum, one-foot wide ladder that would attach to a bumper bracket on

the bottom and lock into the tent base floor at the top. We couldn't afford sleeping bags, so all of our bedding was left in place on top of five or six air mattresses that sat upon a Masonite floor. We slept sardine style and would have to roll over pretty much simultaneously to avoid nighttime skirmishes and wars.

Our sleeping positions stayed pretty much fixed with the three girls in first, Mom next. I was next in line and Dad was last to enter so he could properly secure the opening for the night and to get me up as many times as necessary to avoid a bed wetting incident, which caused serious mayhem on more than one occasion. In hindsight, my bed wetting affliction caused some long-term stresses and anxiety for quite a few years and I rarely spent a night out at friends or overnight events. My inventive father came up with a pretty good system for damning the effusive volumes of my bladder so as not to disturb the other sardines and to avoid having to wash and dry copious amounts of laundry and blankets while on the fly. My mother patented the method of drying sundries by securely hanging them from the car radio antenna and other protrusions while on the road. In the arid hot air of the Great Plains our laundry would soon be dry with a freckled assortment of invertebrates that sacrificed themselves for the honor of helping create designer linens.

The morning reenactment and reversal of our evening setup, assuming no nightly urine-laced incident, would find us making breakfast on a trusty Coleman two burner stove, securing the tent in reverse sequence, sliding in the sides and covering the entire six bed parcel with a canvas fitted cover, held down with many separate pieces of one of my dad's greatest inventions, inch wide rubber bands that had been cut from inter tubes.

This inimitable combination of our vagrant family and peculiar sleeping contrivance certainly drew our fair share of observation from other travelers and campers giving my father a great excuse to utilize his zealous gift of gab, relishing the opportunity for explaining our car topper's merits to envious and curious sojourners.

On one unusually late May night while crossing Arizona, my father underestimated the distance between jerkwaters in remote western Arizona, forcing us to set up our sleeper in the dark on some God forsaken desert boondock. My father, who loved functional aftermarket accessories for the car, had installed the foot-long spiral wires on the right side of the car's rocker panels that would give off a melodious, scraping sound when the car became too close to a curb in the act of parallel parking. Our entire entourage, save for my dad, were engaged in serious slumber, when we all were quickly awakened to the sound of dad uttering serious sounds of fright and primal fear, bellowing something about being struck by a rattlesnake.

We were abruptly awakened, flying from the car to rescue him from the hood of the Chevy. We carefully checked his leg for a puncture wound and finding none began to look around the nearby ground for the snake. We soon discovered that the coiled wire warning mechanism for parallel parking was the culprit and would repeat its stealthy faux snake rattling several times in ensuing trips.

Chapter Seven

"On the road again
Goin' places that I've never been
Seein' things that I may never see again
And I can't wait to get on the road again."
Willie Nelson
On the Road Again

The upside, if there could possibly be a positive aspect to the life of a migrant laborer, was the fact that my father would always plan a new route to take us from the cornfields of Iowa to the cherry orchards of Oregon. Having lived in the West for almost 50 years,

I have revisited many of the tourist attractions that we observed during our pilgrimages of the 40's and 50's on our trips to and from the fruit fields of the northwest.

Dad was also a hopelessly addicted fisherman so our pathway usually led through Yellowstone National Park, where we would rent an aluminum boat and go trolling for cutthroat trout on Yellowstone Lake. We would usually spend at least one part of a day and camp out one evening in the park, giving us a chance to catch a bunch of fish.

Bears were in far greater supply in the park than they are today, so we would see numerous bears crossing highways and in the campgrounds milling around and breaking into coolers, tents and garbage cans. Bears and their errant behavior were much more tolerated than they are now when a misbehaving bear that gets a bit too friendly finds itself on the wrong end of a rifle. Some late May trips through the park would often greet us with copious amounts of snow and very cold weather forcing my frugal father to forgo camping from the car and rent one of the small, log cabins at Fishing Bridge. We could barely afford the four-dollar per night charge and would always rent a one-room, three single bed cabin that was heated by a pot-bellied stove comfortably stoked by firewood that we would scrounge for in the surrounding woodlands. Most of us

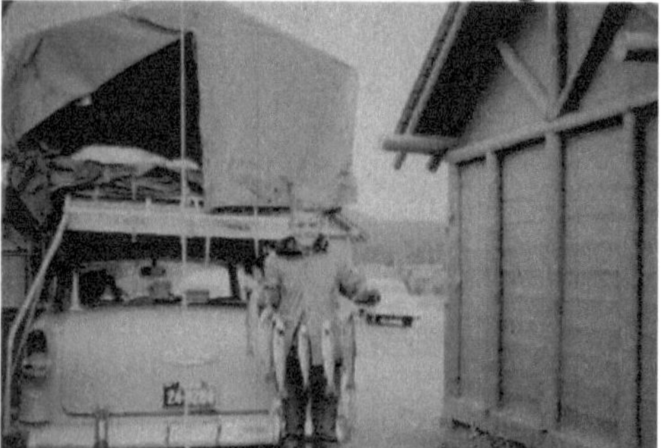

ended up with a bed, though likely shared with a sibling, but being the only lad in the group, I usually ended up on the cabin floor astride a leaky air mattress.

If the fortuitous draw of our cabin location favored our stay, we would be close to the bathroom facilities making for a short, nighttime spree to the john in the bear-infested darkness. Bathroom facility was a charitable description of the accommodations that were there for our relief. They had screened openings above head level for ventilation, no heat, and one lonely light bulb for illumination. They did have flushing toilets in most of the units and sinks with only very cold running water.

Possessing severe stage fright when taking care of business in public restrooms, I always found it very disconcerting to be on display for cluster pees and even more unsettling to be sitting on the john in a door-less crapper with an audience impatiently waiting for their turn. If ever I could find a reason for being a bed wetter, it could possibly have come from choosing a nice easy warm (at least for a brief few minutes) flow into my pj's and sheets to avoid that unnerving trip to the Yellowstone outhouses.

Traveling with six people in a very packed car for four or five days at a crack had its challenges and limitations. Each of us was restricted to bringing a small parcel of personal possessions for our individual edification and entertainment. Needless to say, we were very inventive when the novelty of our one book, card games or other simple playthings lost their appeal. We knew the look and model of every make of car, the color and appearance of every license plate in the nation and played games of chance on any number of things, like picking a specific color of automobiles that we would meet on the road and getting into vicious counting wars on who could count the first one hundred cars of their color first. Or, going through all the words of the alphabet in order, by finding those letters on passing autos, road signs and billboards.

It seemed like it was always hot while traveling, obviously before the days of air conditioning. We had no cooler filled with cold pop or water, because we neither had room for a cooler nor money to buy sodas. We almost always traveled with the windows wide open until the advent of the bullet-shaped, water-filled air capturing window inserts. These contraptions were about two feet in length and about 10 inches in diameter with a reservoir for water and a fan that turned in proportion to the car's velocity, expectantly blowing the water-cooled air into the vehicle while moving. They seemed to perform fairly well as long as the water held out which was usually a fraction of the amount of time that expired between gas fill ups. If you happened to be riding shotgun and could stick you face directly in front of the opening, you could experience a small measure of relief, but the other five red riders suffered the dregs of being on the short end of R.H.I.P., stuffed together in a small space, only made more cozy by the closed windows and cranially-blocked single source of cool, fresh air.

During the at-home months from our annual jaunts my mother was a part time employee at the Hested Lee department store in Denison. In the months leading up to our departure across the fruited plain, she would collect comic books that would normally be sent back to the publisher after not selling. The store manager and family friend, Jim Lambert, would allow my mom to keep all of those comic books, sans the torn-off back covers for our consumption while en route.

She would stash them in every conceivable nook inside of our Chevy. And, we would take turns reading the varied subject/character volumes of comics for as long as they would last. Lack of ample storage space would limit our inventory to about three days of reading, after which we would resort to our sibling bickering, boring games and ubiquitous queries of 'how much further?' I became a major fan of Donald Duck comics with a special place in my heart for Uncle Scrooge McDuck and his huge warehouses of money that required a bulldozer to help him move it around, presumably to keep it fresh and to avoid spontaneous combustion. It may not have been so curious that Scrooge was such a preferred character in that the wages of a lowly migrant worker created benign aspirations for future financial goals.

At summer's end all of our old comic books were kept in boxes and stored for some later mysterious use. Many years later when we finally moved from Denison, thousands of old comic books were stored in our childhood playhouse along with some other items that lacked enough value to haul to our new home in Colorado, but of enough value to be saved from a trip to the city dump. Many years later, I made a visit to our old homestead specifically to retrieve the comic books and an old brass bed for the purpose of reselling them only to discover that someone else obviously knew of their intrinsic value; they were all missing. I was prompted for a visit to the old playhouse after attempting to buy a couple of the old favorite comic books at a memorabilia shop only to find that the two or three that I had selected totaled about $500 in retail value. They were quickly returned to the shelf.

From a child's perspective the annual trip from Denison, Iowa, to The Dalles, Oregon, seemed like it took the same amount of time that the pioneers took in their covered wagons to cross the prairies. Following our initial year, the arrival at our destination of our first orchard in Oregon would be amazingly filled with anticipation. For miles and days crossing four or five large states we pondered about the prospects of the cherry crop, which other families would return from previous summers and what our living accommodations would be for that season.

Later in life, travels with my own family and even later with my grandchildren were radically different in that we stayed in motels, usually with swimming pools.

Or we would travel in a small RV, equipped with a flushing toilet, microwave, electric lights, heater, television, and great beds.

Chapter Eight

*"You worked from can to can't
From when you can see in the morning
Until you can't see at night."*
John and Ruby Lomax
Long Hot Summer Days

T he orchard that we would help harvest in The Dalles was a huge orchard of over 350 acres with thousands of large cherry trees to harvest. Many of the trees were 20 plus feet tall and would produce as much as a half-ton of cherries. Most of the fruit pickers in those days were migrant laborers who followed fruit and produce harvesting year-round, all across the fruited plain, taking them to many different states as the harvest schedules demanded.

Most were Caucasian and descendants of the dust bowl families from Arkansas, Oklahoma, and California. Almost none were Hispanic, a complete

antithesis of today. Our family was the anomaly to all of the people with whom we labored. We only worked with them in the summer months while they moved throughout the year to follow the various seasons and harvests and their children almost never attended school. Depending on their accents and home bases we had clever names for the various groups calling them Arkies, Okies, and bindlestiffs, who were people, mostly single men who traveled with just a bed roll and the clothes on their back, often in boxcars. The large orchard in Oregon owned by the Dave Pink family was one of the better working venues in that harvest location, one of the largest cherry producing areas of the world with thousands of acres of cherry orchards. Our sojourn at the Pinks would usually last for the entire month of June and into early July.

Dave and his wife, Barbara were wonderful people to work for and provided accommodations that were livable. I use the word livable loosely, but in no way to

disparage the Pinks. Most owners would set up rows of canvas wall tents and there was no running water or electricity and old fetid outdoor toilets. At the Pink's orchard there was an enormous packing barn that other than harvest time stored equipment, harvest ladders, wood boxes for hauling harvested cherries and other related gear. It was two stories in height and Dave would provide canvas tarps that we would hang with roping to sequester our designated living spaces, providing sparse separation from 10 or so other families.

Beds were fashioned by suspending coiled springs on the four corners of cherry boxes that were fairly sturdy wooden cartons that were approximately 14 X 24 by 8 inches. There was a supply of mattresses that were roughly the sizes of the open springs and they would become our beds for the next month. Tables and chairs were also formulated from the ubiquitous cherry boxes and were the preferred (and only) furniture of the masses. But, they did vary in appearance and artistic quality by the various names that were stenciled on the sides reflecting the company names of the large fruit packing companies, like Libby, McNeil & Libby, McMinniman and others whose names I don't recall. We could use as many boxes as were needed for our bed frames, for chairs and for shelves and table supports. On rare occasions when we had a few spare moments, my sisters and I would build grand structures with the empty crates, creating rooms, window openings, doors, and furniture. One such architectural phenomenon was named by us, The Rat Hole Motel.

The geography of The Dalles' cherry orchards was extremely hilly and the earth below the rows of cherry trees was completely void of any vegetation, and stayed very dry during harvest. To say that dust was our constant companion and the bane of eyes and ears and general housekeeping could not properly describe its presence. The dust gave new meaning to 'getting our roughage' as it permeated our food and drinks. And so, our summer began in early June sharing a barn-like facility with eight or ten family groups separated only by dusty canvas partitions and a congenial effort to persevere.

We would arise in total darkness awakened by the sounds of hissing Coleman stoves and gas lanterns and the dusk warblings of common laborers getting ready to lay into another day.

The packing house and central area was pretty much the geographical center of the expanse of various species of cherry trees. The sentinels of trees had Arlington cemetery-like rows running for over a mile in each compass heading. The precipitous landscape required stout transportation vehicles to haul pickers, ladders, and harvested crates to and from the hub. If we embarked on the day early enough we could catch a ride to our previous day's stopping point on a large, flatbed trailer pulled along with a D-9 Caterpillar tractor lazily inching its way through its self-created dust bowl, the faceted steel rotating tracks squealing their displeasure and lack of oil.

The first cherries were picked well before the morning sun would rise to join and roast us, eventually making the day nearly unbearable. We were paid by the pound and each box was laboriously weighed when full, and credited to the picker whose number was left with the crate. Each day was 10 to 12 hours in length and physically challenging. Roughly a fourth of the tree could be harvested from the ground, the upper section with the aid of tripod ladders that looked like giant praying mantises of varying heights. The highest altitudes were harvested utilizing a long wooden extension ladder. Each tree had to be completely picked and a scattered handful of cherries were all that remained when we would methodically move to the next tree in line.

Depending on the fruit market conditions we would agree upon a fixed per-pound amount, usually between three and a half to five cents per pound. On a given day we could harvest between two to three hundred pounds per person so our family might earn 80 to 90 dollars a day and as much as a hundred twenty if everything went well. My dad usually thought big in our daily harvest goals, while my sisters and I invented as many diversions as possible that leaned more to a dallying pace.

If you are having any illusions about the pastoral setting of cherry orchards or the romantic nature of fruit tramping, harvesting cherries is a difficult occupation. Most of the day is spent standing on ladders as high as 25 feet above the ground. The picker is clothed with long sleeve shirts and coveralls to protect their skin from sharp branches, wasps, and the sun.

Cherries grow on trees in clusters, called spurs that  might have as many as six to eight cherries. The picker must grab one or more of the stems and with a snap, separate the group from the group from its spur. It was mandatory to leave the spur attached to the limb for the next year's tree health and production. Care must be taken to harvest the cherries with the stem attached to preserve the freshness as they go from tree to bucket, to box, to packing house, and finally to the processing plant. After a few days one's forefingers start to split from the constant force of the stem separating. The picker then wraps forefingers and thumbs with medical tape to protect split and bleeding fingers.

The harvester wears a harness that crosses at the center of the back, and through which he places his arms. The front of the harness has two snap hooks that attach to a concave harvest bucket that sets just above stomach level to contain the cherries. Those buckets  are generally 20 to 30 quarts in size and are thus emptied many times a day into the cherry boxes, requiring many trips up and down the ladders to empty the load. Once a box is filled with roughly 40 to 50 pounds of cherries, another empty box is stacked on top and filled until five or six are stacked in vertical columns.

Many of the larger trees can produce as much as 1500 pounds to a ton of cherries, so leaving 40 to 60 full crates at a harvested tree is not uncommon. The trees have to be cleanly harvested leaving very few cherries for the birds or fruit flies. One large tree could take a good part of the day to harvest with four or five people having to move their ladders numerous times.

The ladders were all made of wood and of two types of design. Most of the ladders were tripod in design with two legs supporting the steps and a third leg, attached at the top by a hinged bracket that was extended to create a three-point stance. The closer the third leg was to the steps, the more vertical was the ladder's incline. They were 10, 12, 16 and 18 feet in height and weighed around 30 to 50 pounds. When all of us had ladders positioned around a tree, it had the appearance of very large grasshoppers attacking the tree. Moving a ladder required pulling the third leg so it was adjacent to the step portion, putting a shoulder under a step and moving it to a strategic location within reaching distance of as many cherries as possible, and then extending the third leg to give it balance.

Moving the longer versions required strength and balance to avoid losing the vertical position above your body and having the ladder topple over into the tree or on top of someone. Once positioned, the picker would pick as they went vertically and then come down with each full bucket. At the upper final portion of the position it was often necessary to stand on the very top rung to reach cherries still above your location. We also employed the use of five-foot-long stiff wire hooks that allowed the picker to hook on to a branch and pull it inward to access its fruit.

For fruit above the reaches of the tripods it required the use of a ladder called a 'spike.' It was a 24 to 28-foot-long extension like ladder with the two side rails forming a point at the top for easy insertion into a tree fork or against a mass of limbs. My mom and my baby sister when she was still young, were the recipients of access to the 'low hanging fruit,' and were allowed to do all of the harvesting from ground level. That expression has a profound meaning to those who have been fruit tree harvesters. My next oldest sister, Bess was the most aggressive and tough and, along with me and my dad would do the crazy, upper stuff. She was also my music buddy and we liked similar transistor radio concerts while we worked.

At times, certain species of cherries deemed too ripe or others that were destined for the maraschino process could be harvested without the stems. The process was called 'glomming,' and was the delight of pickers because one could harvest 30 to 40 percent more than doing so with the stems intact. By the end of a glomming day ones' hands would be stained and sticky with the juices going a fair distance up one's arm.

Harvest days always began at first light and would usually conclude around five p.m. with a short break to eat lunch. Cherries are only grown in geographic locations that provide very dry climates during the harvest. Any moisture in the form of rain when cherries are ripe is the certain kiss of death for a crop. Rain drops settle into the cavity where the stem attaches to the cherry and eventually will seep into the cherry causing it to split from a combination of its own sugars and the added volume of water. Consequently, the desired climate for picking time is always dry and arid and usually quite hot. By the end of the day, a picker is usually coated with dust from the vegetation free earth, sticky from the juices, and soaked in sweat from the full body covering and the heat.

Picking cherries is repetitive, mind numbing, and pretty simple, without much need for concentration. It is easy to get radically bored and much of the day is spent dreaming of what a summer should be, telling and retelling old stories, jawing with nearby families, and doing whatever one can to help pass the time.

Our major form of entertainment was from a small transistor radio, the prehistoric version of an iPod with its small, one speaker serving the audio appetites of each of us. It would be set on a frequency that barely absorbed enough radio waves to consistently hear an entire song. Other than that electronic wonder, we had to be pretty inventive to muddle through the dreariness of a long day in the sun.

The one visual perk of working in that area was an ever present view of Mount Hood to the south and of Mount Adams to the north of us in Washington. As the sun would move across its rhythmic sweep, the multi-hued vibrant effect on the snow-covered monoliths would give us pause to tender our artistic impressions of what flavor of ice cream delight they would emulate. They could appear to be chocolate, strawberry, caramel, and other colors depending on the time of day and the sun's angle.

As we would move through the rows and columns of trees we would interact with other families or individuals with whom we labored. This eclectic band of fruit pickers would vary little from year to year and we would wait with anticipation on our trip from Iowa hoping that we would reconnect with our favorites. Some families had children who were more or less in the various age groups of each of us. Our Iowa home friends and acquaintances seemed like fairly dull, normal people in comparison. The entire lot of our nomadic summer friends possessed quirks and idiosyncrasies, individually and collectively and were strange and unusual fascinating people.

Many were interrelated and most called each other by their last name preceded by a brother or sister moniker such as brother Vaughn or sister Brewner. A few of their number were either self-appointed or collectively appointed as their spiritual leaders and were thus preacher Vaughn or preacher Benson primarily followers of the Assembly of God faith. My family was a serious practicing batch of Presbyterians and rarely, if ever, missed a Sunday worship service regardless of where we were traveling or how near we might be from Bum Fart, Nevada, or some other remote podunk settlement. My father and mother would stop at some little town along the way and always manage to get us dressed and ready to stop at whatever congregation that was close enough to our travel path to join in worship with the local believers.

As one of the embellishments to our car-top RV, my father had engineered a storage area that was located just below the rear end of the sleeper/carrier. The unit had some sort of a drawer-like slider system that allowed the two big drawers to extend rearward providing access to our really good Sunday-go-to-meeting duds. We would pull into some shady area in a city park, open up the a moire and before God and anyone else who might be cruising by, get into our Sunday best and head to worship.

In our early years of life, the Presbyterian Church would strongly encourage consistent attendance. The denomination would award a young person with a beautiful, colored, gold inlaid pin for perfect attendance for an entire year. As in, if you missed one

Sunday, no pin. In successive years, a gold wreath around the pin was awarded for year two. Sequential years would have a colored, gold plated bar suspended by gold chain links indicating the number of years of perfect attendance. My medallion numbered 10, perfect attendance from age 7 through 17. Had I kept the streak going through college and beyond, I would likely have avoided many self-inflicted crises and detours.

My hindsight perspective on the issue of faith is that young people in my era were involved because it was the accepted and common thing for almost all families to be involved with their church and to attend regularly.

My reflections on the subject leads me to conclude that the participation level then was very high, but our spiritual depth was somewhat surface level. Over the years it is abundantly clear that the level of engagement is radically diminished, but the depth of faith in our young people who choose that path is profound. I know so many marvelous stories of troubled young people going on a mission trip or working in foster care settings or homeless ministries that have dynamic path corrections.

Chapter Nine

"Take this job and shove it,
I don't work here anymore."
Johnny Paycheck
Take This Job and Shove It

I described some of the challenges of picking cherries because most of a tree's production is well above those that can be picked from the ground. OSHA would likely have a field day if they were to venture into an orchard and observe the harvest process. Over the course of my cherry career, I can recall quite a number of falls, several that happened to me. It was not uncommon for a branch on which we had leaned our ladder to break off causing the picker to quickly grab the tree to avoid a fall. The tripod style ladders were very prone to tipping and either falling toward the tree or away from it. The ground was usually tilled soil, almost always on a slant and relatively soft, making a landing less perilous, but descending through the tree had its pitfalls (pun intended).

When someone had a ladder mishap which was fairly common, the rest of the family would briefly take a look to see if there was serious damage and respond with the well-worn phrase, "I hope you didn't spill your cherries." Another hazard was reaching into a clump of cherries and mistakenly grabbing a hornet's nest. That was common enough that harvest crews would scan all of the trees that were on the next day's harvest list and look for nests. When discovered, we would go out after dark with a quart sized tin can filled with rags and white gas, light it and slide it over the nest when all of the residents were tucked away for the evening. However, in thickly vegetated trees they were easy to miss.

On one such occasion when we were in the Flathead Lake harvest, I was up on a spike ladder, some 20 feet up when I grabbed a nest and was instantly stung. My reaction caused me to fall through the tree and land with a thud. With over 60 stings on my face, neck, hands, and arms I quickly went into anaphylactic shock. We were some 40 miles from Polson, Montana, and the nearest hospital. My dad put me in the car and drove me there where I received the necessary injections to keep me ticking. I was a hurting lad for a few days.

Another subtle, no-so-pleasant occurrence was for small airplanes to fly over the orchards with crop dusting applications. It was always a novelty to watch their skill as they followed the steep contours of the orchards while dropping their load. The stuff had a very toxic smell and when they got real close it sometimes gave us headaches or upset stomachs. When my dad inquired about its composition he was told that it was harmless and would not have any lasting effects on humans. Think Teflon. We later found out that the liquid vapor was a compound known as Malathion, used to protect the ripe cherries from fruit fly, which can be devastating to a cherry crop. Not too many studies existed in those days to assess the effects of chemicals on humans. Except for my parents we are all still alive and relatively lucid, so maybe the concern was innocuous.

It was also fairly common to find rattlesnakes slithering through an orchard or camped out beneath the cherry boxes. On one such occasion, a nearby picker picked up an empty crate in which to dump his pail when a rattler struck at him. The fangs entered the cuff of his shirt and the snake could not extricate himself from the shirt. Fortunately, the fangs did not penetrate through the fabric or enter his wrist, but it made for some real excitement.

Another potential hazard was poison oak and ivy. I managed somehow to get into some ivy. For a while, I just thought it was an insect bite or a rash, but as I scratched at it, it managed to spread and eventually covered my entire body (yes, there also). In spite of the collective wisdom offerings of a bunch of fruit pickers from varied cultural and ethnic backgrounds, it continued to consume my flesh. One bright soul suggested a good old fashioned, not the drink, sunburn. So I found a secluded space and spent the good part of a day frying my skin. Within a few days and a lot of pain, the ivy was put to death.

Chapter Ten

My father was a very spiritual man raised by parents who had very puritanical beliefs who espoused tea totalism, forswore swearing, and condoned very little that could be construed as fun. Today his brand of faith would likely be dubbed as legalism, which is defined as a brand of faith that has little room for frivolity and espouses following all of the commandments and rules with little margin for dalliance.

His strong belief system was such that he insisted that we never miss worship on the Sabbath. He was also charismatic enough that he could stroll into a strange church in an even stranger town with his family in tow and feel like he belonged. We would languish long after the service while he would regale the local believers with stories of our travels and of our family. He expressed great pride in each one of us and would brag about our cherry-harvesting prowess.

He would always introduce each one of us and make it clear that we all had single syllable names which was much easier for behavior corrections as most parents seem to get sibling names mixed up when chastising for abhorrent behavior.

I have some fond memories of some places of worship, but a few really stand out. Our fellow fruit pickers were mostly a reverent lot and liked practicing their brand of religion without the adornments of pious buildings with steeples and stained glass windows and without the guidance of an ordained or, for that matter, a trained pastor.

They would graciously invite us to come get saved and cleansed along with them right there in the packing shed. My father would always decline and we would dress up, and head down the dusty road to a church in the town near where we were working. The children of preacher Vaughn and of brothers and sisters Brewner and the other families were fairly persistent with their invitations to join with them. One particular Sunday evening, my parents suggested that we join them, but they opted out for their own brand of fervor and left the four of us to join the faithful at the assembly in the packing shed.

We very innocently joined in and felt like we were holding our own, singing along, knowing some of the songs and faking others that we didn't know. Preacher Vaughn gave a sermon that seemed pretty docile and followed up with some fervent praying the likes of which we had never experienced.

We bowed our heads and kneeled on the splintered wood floors as the preacher-led prayer began. He chastened others to join in and to bring their petitions and praises so that the entire group could participate in their pleas and their vexations. Their responses were forthcoming and plentiful and soon the room was a cacophony of crescendo voices wailing and supplicating to our Almighty. From our genuflecting pose we each sneaked a peak at each other to confirm our extreme level of discomfort. We weren't quite sure how to respond as none of us had been schooled in fervent prayer, speaking in tongues, or being slain in the Spirit.

I don't recall who was the first to bolt, but that decision was one of the few unanimous agreements of our childhood days. When my parents returned they were amused at what we had observed and apparently had a fairly good idea of what we might encounter. Later that evening I think we were all amazed that the brethren returned to a somewhat normal demeanor and that no one had expired on the packing house floor. First Presbyterian Church, The Dalles, Oregon, never looked so good the following Sunday morning. As mid-century pubescents, we had clever names for faith denominations different from our own. They were Cat lickers, JW's, Holy Roller, Baptistas and others, but after our little sojourn that June Sunday, Holy Rollers had a very laconic, pithy ring to it and clearly described the participation of people actually rolling on the floor.

Because religion was such a prolonged and mandatory part of my early life I had become somewhat ambivalent about it when I left high school. I didn't contemplate much about my need for it in my life or about being absent from it. When I began matriculating at CU, religion was pushed to a back burner. For most of my extended years in college, I had a great excuse not to go. One of my college jobs was delivering newspapers for the *Denver Post* on a rural motor route, driving some 50 miles a day. Sunday morning deliveries began at about 3:00 a.m. lasting until about 7:00. After Saturday night fraternity socializing, I was usually in rough shape to drive my route and to stay awake, and then come home to get ready for church. I became a fairly consistent drop out and seemed to get by just fine without the ritual of Sunday morning worship.

I know that was tough on my dad, but he didn't say much about it and would on occasion mention that it would be nice for me to join them on Sunday morning, and from time to time I would accept their offer. In a recent men's study group that I have been a participant of for over 40 years, we studied a book by Timothy Kelly, _Making Sense of God,_ one chapter entitled "Is it Reasonable to Believe in God?" helped me to understand the evolution of my faith from its early years of perfect attendance, to abandonment and then to full-on dependence on a greater power. I think that most humans would agree that either God exists or there is no such thing. My fuzzy thinking lens was wiped clean by reading astronomer and quantum physicists and their complex descriptions of the perfect balance of the universe where if just one minor thing among a billion trillion was not dialed in, we would not exist.

After exiting college and searching for meaningful pathways, I began the job search, the partner search, the spiritual search and discovered how important it was to find a life partner who was on the same sacred page. I went to a church in my hometown that was close to the university with a lot of attending coeds. I eventually found the love of my life, got married at that same church, had three daughters who were baptized there and kindled by the youth ministry. As soon as my family came along, it all began to make sense when I realized how fearful it would be and how inadequate I was to raise a family along with my wife on my own credentials and pedigree. Once again, I was locked in and have been, without discontent ever since.

As a journalist, I have always avoided using cliches whenever I am writing. Expressing my feelings about my association with a church body is a challenge to scribe without using Christian cliches, but I will give it a go. Over the years, like all people, I have had small and large group associations: college friends, high school buddies, military fox hole brothers, college fraternity mates, families with whom we raised our children, business associates, etc. All of humanity for the most part has similar, but maybe different connections.

A church family either from a small group, a local church or a denomination, or the entire family of Christ followers provides a guaranteed life source if one were to seek it when and wherever we might find ourselves in crisis mode. Throughout my life I have experienced several misfortunes that could easily have derailed my family...a car wreck, a medical diagnosis, premature death of a parent, investment stupidities, crisis with a child or grandchild. In all cases when I needed a spiritual recharge, the church body never failed to deliver. A simple Bible verse, a lyric from a song, a phone call can lift an empty spirit in a desperate time. All of my other old associations faded away and were inconsequential during the valley of shadows.

I can only surmise that the religious investment that my parents had made in my formative years eventually brought sunshine after the storms of life. Part of the book title "A Thousand Rainbows," might be an exaggerated number, but if I began to chronicle the fog to sunshine events along the way, this book would be far too large, but the sum of 1,000 wouldn't be much off the mark.

Chapter Eleven

"Remember the breakwaters down by the wave
I first found my courage knowing daddy would save
I could hold back the tide
with my dad by my side."
Peter Gabriel
Father, Son

For much of my early life, I believed that my father and I were miles apart on just about any subject. I very much respected him and always felt that there was a behavioral line in the sand that I would never choose to cross. I got close to that line on hundreds of adventures, but never over it. It wasn't because I feared him, but because of my respect for him that I completely hid most of my teen and college indiscretions from him. When living with my parents on and off during my college years, I awoke with the 'flu' more times that I can count, and I don't think that he ever suspected that I was hungover, because he had never observed the symptoms or experienced them himself. On a number of occasions, he would suggest for me as a young, male driver to apply for non-drinkers car insurance to save a lot on car insurance premiums. Not.

He was a great provider, a lover of my mother and his family and a schoolteacher and basketball coach for most of his short life. He went to college to become an osteopathic physician, but got short circuited after one year of pre-med when the great depression caused his father's bank to fail, cutting off his college funding. He settled for a degree in education and became a teacher.

His last job as a teacher in 1953 mysteriously ended without cause when he was replaced by a man who was a country clubber, golfer, and good old boy. My dad never fit into that class. His last year's income as a teacher was $5,400.00. Thus, the need for our summer escapades.

He was also a craftsman and handyman and could fix just about anything that needed it. I spent many hours alongside him learning how to fix broken house stuff and cars, antiques, and whatever else needed repair. He died at the age of 61 after suffering a stroke and three previous heart failures. Reflecting on his life and what I remember of his character, personality, and traits, I realize how many pieces of his DNA that I acquired. I dreaded what he cooked up for our summers, but I later realized that he was in survival mode. He refused to accept any form of government or other assistance and eked out a plan to make it all work.

On many occasions I observed in him what I thought were digestive, stomach issues, only to inherit the same anxiety traits that were really the cause of his distress, and on many occasions, the reason for my own. His list, my list: family first, faithfulness, anxiety, frugality, hospitality, generosity, heart disease, tools for toys, used cars, fixing cars, helping neighbors, church elder, upland hunter, fisherman, athlete, coach, a husband to the same woman for life, father.

During the ensuing years of my life, I have reflected on the blessings of such rich DNA and how it has molded me as a parent and grandparent. I never condemned errant behavior from any of my progeny because it never reached the level of my own dalliances. There have been many times when I would start being judgmental only to come to the conclusion and reflection of 'been there, done that' awareness. One of my big regrets is that my father didn't live long enough for me to express all of the above thoughts and thankfulness for him, to him, or for him to have lived long enough to see that I turned out ok.

Looking through the prism of three generations of my family, I can clearly see a thread and spool of bloodline and how clearly much of it is passed along, either to take credit for or lay the blame on or for accolades or deficiencies that the gene pool has shared. While watching my father display some of the unfortunate side effects caused by anxiety over many years, we were always told that he was suffering from ulcers. I am not sure that stress and anxiety in the 40's and 50's were properly identified and other causes were usually blamed.

When I look at this man, my father from a position of being in his shoes, I am not sure I would have managed a family of six on a $5,000/year salary, buying a home, owning a car, planning for our college, and keeping us all clothed, fed, and healthy. He always labeled our summer jaunts to pick fruit as an adventure and full of fun. But, I know it was his disclaimer to avoid verbalizing that our fruit picking adventures were really a means of financial survival and drudgery.

Chapter Twelve

"Oh brothers, let's go down
Let's go down, come on down
Come on, brothers, let's go down
Down in the river to pray"
Alison Krauss
Down to the River to Pray

From the time I was seven years old through my second year in college I spent my summers in this same venue. Summer after summer I would pile into the family car-turned-RV and head for the cherry orchards of the West. With a few exceptions pretty much the same harvest crew would show up as faithfully as the swallows of Capistrano at the precise time to begin harvesting in Oregon and then on to Washington state and then Montana spending pretty nearly a month at each location until the harvests were completed.

Of all of my acquaintances throughout my life, few were more colorful and memorable than some of the associates on our picking crews and also a few of the owners. Most traveled with their family year-round and the children were often uneducated or at best spent little time in a classroom. If they had any home base it was usually Lodi or Live Oak, California where they might settle for three or four months at a time for a succession of varying fruit and vegetable harvest times.

Working ten to twelve hour days left little time for socializing or merriment. After a full day of physically demanding labor we would race for the packing shed and the two outdoor but enclosed solar showers that likely were some of the very earliest contraptions of green, ecologically correct water heating. Hot water from blackened storage tanks supported on the roof of the shower stalls would cascade over the first dozen or so early queues and then the water temps would taper down so that the stragglers would have a very quick, unpleasant tepid splash.

Following the brief interlude in the rustic spa, my mom would fire up the Coleman stove with its manually pressurized air and a match to light it up. The stove had only two burners each with a cooking pot nested over the flame, containing some quickly prepared brew that varied each evening, but was repeated every second or third day. Slumgullion stew, macaroni and cheese and a hamburger mixed with either corn or some vegetables would be quickly inhaled by six hungry farm hands, but not until we had together uttered our pre-meal liturgy, *"Thank you Father for all the blessings that thou dost give, direct and guide our daily paths and teach us how to live. In Jesus' name we pray, Amen."* I likely repeated that same prayer at least five or six thousand times during the early course of my life and have often questioned my sincerity in visualizing the meaning of the words, but never doubting God's part in delivering on our petitions.

Leftovers were a yet-to-be created word in the vocabulary of our small crew and the food and the mealtime fellowship and chatter had a short lifespan. We would retire to the R and R part of our day for as long as our tired bodies would endure. Considering a 4:00 a.m. wakeup call from our father, the evening festivities were short and succinct. One of my favorite authors, Edward Abbey, scribed it, working *"from darkness till darkness."* We would often socialize with the other picking crew members and some were entertainers in an eclectic way. A few played instruments, usually harmonicas and accordions and others were great raconteurs of stories from <u>The Grapes of Wrath</u> days of their lives.

Others could be wildly entertaining simply by displaying personalities unlike any we had ever met. One man, Henry Ulmer was an alcoholic and would get pretty hammered every night until he passed out, but very amusing up to that point. I had never been around a drinking person before as my father espoused the theory that one could never become an alcoholic without taking a first drink. Hank would drink cheap jug wine until he claimed to see snakes and other demons. His father, Fred Ulmer was a decent, older man who was the complete antithesis of his son and he would patiently wait for the inevitable carnage and then drag his son off to bed.

Oftentimes Hank would drink enough at night to carry over through the early morning hours and he would fall off of his ladder or pass out beneath the cherry tree. My dad cited him as a prime example for the sins of excessive alcohol consumption.

Each of us would gravitate toward other young people our age and would become quite good friends, considering that we would only see them again one year hence for the period of a month or two. Preacher Vaughn had a couple of sons, one of which I befriended. Larry latched on to me so that he could secretly borrow some of our huge inventory of comic books. He couldn't read very well, but he liked a chance to understand the story by its progression of the colorful graphics.

Larry had two other brothers. One, Leon was the same age as my oldest sister, Ann. By the time she was 15 or so in our fifth or sixth season of summer bliss she and Leon became quite an item. I think Leon had the serious hots for Ann as they would head off to the orchard together for what I thought must be some amorous harmony. When the season ended at The Dalles, they were always hoping that both families would end up at the same orchard for our next harvest.

Summer's end would lead to some sporadic letter writing, the contents of which I was not privy. Eventually the romance ended as most, long distance, star-crossed liaisons do.

One of the most interesting characters in our group was John McaFee, a true hobo in every sense of the word.

Chapter Thirteen

John Scott McaFee, "Scotty," was certainly one of the most interesting persons I had or have ever met. He and our family sort of adopted each other I think mostly out of sympathy for him from my Mother and his need for familial companionship from us. He appeared on one of the first days of the first years of our fruit-picking careers. He happened to be picking on a row next to ours and came over during a smoke break and introduced himself. He was very amiable and had enough of a sense of humor that we were all ears and eyes at his antics and appearance. He was mostly bald and had a number of gold teeth that contrasted starkly with the tobacco stained remainder of his chops. He had a number of tattoos on his muscled body and he was noticeably bow legged. His hands were huge like a dairy farmer who milked his own cows and he had enormous veins that snaked along his arm like ropes. Like most fruit pickers his hands were pretty gnarly, with numerous cracks at the edges of his fingernails. When someone would compliment him on his physique he would oftentimes remove his shirt curl up his forearm to show off his biceps and display a grin that reminded me of a chimpanzee. Before long we

already knew a few of his earlier career paths and he regaled us with stories of his cowboy days, time in the Army in WWII, his stint as a wildcatter on oil rigs and of his hobo days, riding the rails of America and living off the fat of the land. Little did we know in that early encounter the full extent of his colorful past, but those stories would soon unfold and be oft repeated over the years of our friendship with him.

My mother took a platonic liking to him and sort of adopted him into our family partly because of her propensity to take care of strays and partly because he was pretty amusing and I suspected, lonely. In subsequent years he began showing up on our doorstep in Iowa for weeks at a time and would stay in Denison with our family during some of the off time from harvest seasons.

Scotty pretty much followed the crop harvest schedule of a number of different fruits and produce for nine months of the year and would then spend his winters in Quartzsite, Arizona, prospecting for gold. He was generous to our family and would give some lavish gifts to my mother and sisters. On one such excursion to Iowa, he gave each of them a set of earrings and matching necklaces that he fashioned from pure gold that was encapsulated in an oil-filled, transparent carrier. Each carrying pure flakes of gold containing an ounce.

He took a particular liking to my youngest sister, Jane and always displayed a bit-over the-top-affection for her that today would likely be frowned upon or

questioned. He would buy even better gifts for her, once gracing her with a complete western style clothing setup replete with fringed leather jacket, skirt, cowboy boots and Stetson all matching in color. He always referred to her as his princess. In our later assessment of this adoration we surmised that he may have had a young daughter in his earlier days that he had somehow lost. In his autobiographical accounting of his life there were many obvious chronological gaps that he would never talk about, especially if it was about his family.

When we first met Scotty his mode of transportation

was a Willys Jeep wagon with four-wheel drive. He had it set up so that he could sleep and cook in it with a fairly innovative and elaborate design. He claimed that the Jeep had over two-hundred thousand miles and would always lament its possible inability to make it to his next destination. One year he showed up in The Dalles with the same old Jeep, but pulling a small trailer that had to be one of the first camping style trailers.

To caravan from place to place with him was a tedious experience for us even though our old car top  camper Chevy wasn't exactly a race car. It seemed anyway that our trips from Iowa west or from state to state between harvests took forever, but traveling with Scotty was snail-like in comparison. He always described going over some of the mountain passes as if it were a mountaineering challenge on foot and was just about as slow. Top speed going up or down a pass was around ten to fifteen mph and many times we would have to stop due to an overheated engine, wait for the steam to dissipate and then replenish the radiator with coolant. One or two of us would often ride along with him for company, giving him a chance to expound on one of his well-worn stories and endure the smoke from his hand rolled cigarettes and the rankness of his spitting can.

One of his favorite family pleasers when we were encamped was his creation of his gourmet southern fried pies. I've often thought about Googling that name to see what might appear and what the ingredients consisted of, but I can assure you that they were a delight. They were sort of light flaky croissant-like pastry filled with a pureed fruit concoction. They were a to-die-for magnum opus. When we complimented him on his cooking genius he would launch into a story of his days as a gourmet chef in a French restaurant during his days in Europe before the story would end with his usual career-ending life threatening catastrophe forcing him to change in his career path; in this case a kitchen explosion that nearly killed him.

Scotty was as faithful returning to spending the summers with our family as the leaves reappearing on deciduous trees. In the years following the end of our summer journeys, my sister Jane and her husband Bill made a few visits to his 'mining camp' in Quartzsite and always found him to be in good spirits and still dabbling in sluice box mining for gold.

On one such trip in the early 90's, he was nowhere to be found. They did some research with the local archive keepers only to find that he had passed from heart failure and was buried in a lonely spot in a graveyard near where he spent his winters. Although a loner for most of his life, he developed enough relationships with his bindlestiff friends to be honored with a memorial service, a grave site, and a headstone.

Chapter Fourteen

"Take me to the river, drop me in the water
Push me in the river, dip me in the water
Washing me down, washing me"
Talking Heads
Take Me to the River

Brother Brewner, the Chief, was another character that helped bring some amusement to our laborious days. He was a full blooded Native American who was born very near The Dalles, Oregon. He and his family of five were pretty much year round migrants and enjoyed coming back to The Dalles for the summer harvest as it was kind of a homecoming. His son, Chebonney, was my age and we hit it off pretty well. I was always hoping to learn some real Indian stuff from him, but disappointed that he was about as much like the melting pot of American life as I was.

On some evenings the Chief would be visited by members of the local Celilo tribe and it would be a colorful and entertaining time. Again I was hoping for some authentic Indian stuff to happen, but they would pretty much hang out like the rest of us and spoke the same language that we all spoke. Occasionally, some of the Chief's friends or family would bring along a few jugs of Thunderbird wine and the party atmosphere would change. Still, no ethnic dancing or warrior stuff, just mellow, low key inebriation.

In the late 50's before the construction of The Dalles dam on the Columbia River, Celilo Falls was still a scenic wonder and tourist attraction. The falls rivaled Niagara Falls for their majesty and awe. Perhaps not as high as Niagara, they extended across the entire width of the Columbia River and created their own weather zone simply by the mist and fog that rose from the cascading waters of the Columbia. At that time there were no water impoundments all the way from the Pacific Ocean upstream to the John Day dam some seventy or so miles further upstream. The Columbia had prolific Salmon runs that would begin in June and run through late summer.

The Celilo Indians had exclusive rights to harvest the fish any way that they chose either by fishing gear or by netting. In the low water months, they built elaborate, but insanely unsafe wooden ladder systems from the rim of the river down to where they would hover just above the cresting water. The infrastructure of the ladders was attached to the cliffs of the riverside with spikes, ropes and whatever seemed to suffice for the most part. Some of the story tellers spoke of some ominous misfortunes of the netters. During the salmon runs, brave braves would descend the ladders with large nets that were attached to the end of long poles. They would hang over the edges of the platforms and net the fish as they would make their way up and over the falls in their quest for their spawning grounds. I was truly amazed to watch this process, both for the courage of the men who would risk their lives to catch the fish as well as for the salmon that had such incredible beauty and strength to ascend hundreds of feet of surging, turbulent water to once again find the very point of their own origin.

The Chief would bring large fillets of the Chinooks after they had been smoked and sell them to the picking crew. It was about as savory as any fish I had or have ever eaten.

When the dam was completed in the late 50's not only did it severely hinder the salmon migration, but it took away one of the most incredible natural geologic phenomena of the western United States. Today, fish ladders permit a small fraction of the once prolific Columbia River salmon runs to eke out a meager survival from extinction.

In my latter life, I became very involved with Trout Unlimited, becoming the Boulder Flycasters president for a period of two years. Along with the national organization, we were committed to enhancing the biology and limnology of freshwater rivers and streams. More than once, TU engaged in battle with the myriad of BLM water inpoundments to guarantee minimum streams flows to keep aquatic things alive and passageways around the concrete dams for benefit of the spawning Salmonids.

Chapter Fifteen

"Up in the mornin'
Work like a devil for my pay
But that lucky old sun got nothin' to do
But roll around heaven all day."
Ray Charles
That Lucky Old Sun

I t took roughly a month to complete the harvest at Dave Pink's orchard in The Dalles, but eventually all of the Bing, Royal Anne, Republican, Lambert, and a few other species of cherries would be harvested. It was a bittersweet time as we would likely not see some of our friends for another year. The orchard owners would finish

on the last day after we had all cleaned up and put on fresh clothing with a picnic and watermelon feed and the greatly anticipated pay day.

Our earnings would be held until the harvest was complete so this was a highly anticipated event. During the harvest, swampers would pass by our location, pick up each completed box of cherries with the picker's number inserted, weigh it, and record the weight of each box. The boxes would then be carefully stacked on a flat-bed trailer pulled by a retired Army three-quarter ton jeep. Once it was full, usually four to five tiers high depending on the slope of the orchard, the swamper would then drive the load to the packing shed where the lugs were transferred to a large truck for transport to the packing plants in town. On most days two such loads would be taken in, some twenty to thirty tons of cherries.

Pay day was a big deal for everyone, but for me and my siblings it almost made up for the drudgery of our summertime blues. We each had our own account and stood in line with the rest of the crew waiting our turn to "slop up" as the migrants referred to this event. All payments were in crisp greenbacks and each of us would come away with four to six hundred dollars mostly in hundreds and twenty dollar bills along with a few silver dollars for the odd lots. After saying goodbye to our friends we would head into town for a spending spree, time at the local swimming pool and perhaps a movie that none of us could ever manage to finish without falling asleep.

"Don't let that money burn a hole in your pocket" was the worn cliche that my father predictably articulated to us. And we were pretty safe from going hog wild due to the constraints of space in the old Chevy that would limit our binge to a few new comic books and a few other small personal items.

The next harvest venue in Wenatchee, Washington, usually began around the mid part of July and most of our crew would look for smaller orchards around The Dalles or Hood River, some 50 miles west to fill in the time gap. Rarely, we would end up working with others from Pink's at one of the interim jobs, however, Scotty always joined our family. These fill-in assignments were usually two weeks at the most and were not nearly as fun without the social interactions of a big crew. Dave Pink was always gracious in allowing us to stay at the packing shed if we could find extended work in The Dalles, in which case we would pile into the Chevy each morning before daylight and drive to the job.

The ride was always a treat for all but the chauffeur as we would all extend our sleep time by the length of the trip. Dave Pink's place was three miles from town on Orchard Road. One year we found a job at a small orchard another dozen or so miles up a canyon at the very end of Orchard Road at a place that would remind one of the culture and geography of the movie, *Deliverance*. Frank Segui and his sons owned the place and had forgotten to join the 20th Century. The place had no running water or electricity and was situated in a canyon with a relatively small flat area hacked out between the steep walls of the gorge. Where Dave Pink's orchard was all culled dirt, the Segui's ground beneath the orchard was weed and grass infested. The place was overrun with rattle snakes and robins, the latter doing a serious number on the ripe cherries and their strawberry fields and the former scaring the snot out of all of us by their sudden appearance in and around the trees that we were picking.

The Seguis had many yarns about close calls with the snakes that kept us all on a high level of alertness. Each year they would bring in several neighbors and have a rattlesnake roundup and claimed to take into custody several hundred or more each year. Of course, Scotty told his harrowing experience when a rattlesnake struck at him from a strawberry bush sinking its fangs into the cuff of his shirt. The four-foot long reptile was so deeply embedded that the serpent couldn't extract its fangs nor could Scotty risk pulling it off for fear of a secondary strike so he walked a long distance before he found someone to help cut its head off. The snake had managed to completely penetrate the fabric of his shirt but not his skin and it spewed venom about his wrist, burning his skin and causing numbness. Scotty always claimed, like cats, to have had nine lives and we eventually knew at least that many of his death defying stories.

Prior to our arrival I am not sure who the Seguis had hired to do their harvesting, but they had no method for accounting the quantity of fruit harvested or how to decide what to pay us for our toil, so we borrowed one of Dave Pink's retired scales and had to show them how to use it and what the dial was indicating with each weighed box. The process turned into math and English lessons that may have been their first exposure to either. The usual separate accounting for each one of our family members was an even greater challenge because it brought spelling and writing into this out-of-the-way classroom. Frank Segui's son, Larry seemed to be the oldest and most advanced of the four family members and became the swamper for their harvesting functions.

In the process of assigning each of us a harvest account he had to create a spreadsheet with each of our names along with columns for recording the weight of each completed box and accumulated totals for our eventual slopping up. The spreadsheet was actually a very small spiral notebook that fit conveniently inside of one his bib overall pockets along with the only writing instrument that likely existed at the Segui ranch, a very short, dull pencil stub. I think Larry knew most of the alphabet letters but had difficulty properly lining any sequence of them up in some manner that would spell a word—seriously phonics challenged. So Jane became Hebr, Ann was En, Bess was the closest to the real deal as Bis and I was Cdn, that if one 'sounded it out' came close to Stan. To this day all of us refer to Jane as Heber in our moments of levity or if we are together and sharing war stories of our migrant past.

The only water closet at their ranch was a rickety out house which the Seguis also used for their excretory requirements. Need I say more? The challenge was to try

and hold any number twos from dusk till dawn or go and squat in the weeds with the rattlesnakes. We had to bring our own toilet paper to avoid despoiling a perfectly good Montgomery Ward catalog or their neglected phone book. Scotty would often suggest that we go over and hunker down behind a tree and close our eyes stating that we likely wouldn't see anyone. Driving back to the future at the end of the day allowed us to experience the anachronism of a pioneer museum without the price of admission. Slopping up at the Seguis had its own special meaning and expeditiousness.

Other temporary employment would also lead us to Hood River, Oregon, and then to the small town of Odell, Oregon, to work in smaller orchards there. The area around Hood River had a proliferation of different varieties of fruit and other produce, but being cherry picking specialists we would opt for that preference. The Hood River valley was located on the northern drainage of the Mt. Hood watershed and had a sub alpine geography. It was usually cooler during days that were partially shadowed by the steepness of surrounding terrain. All of the farms in the area were owned by immigrant Japanese families and there was a surprising language barrier when communicating the logistics of harvesting their crop but an improvement over working for Frank Segui. They were fastidious people and their farms and buildings were always immaculate and clean but the higher elevation and the topography coaxed another ten to twenty feet of height from the cherry tree's vertical rise, struggling upward to get enough sunshine and heat to produce fruit.

The Hood River trees however, had to be harvested almost exclusively with extension ladders that would reach as high as forty feet making the access to branches that extend outward from the trunk problematic. There was almost no ground hogging that my mother and youngest sister usually claimed as their exclusive turf where they could harvest as much as a fourth of the trees' yield. We should have earned extra hazard duty pay for the challenge of picking fruit that was so inaccessible.

The upside of working in the valley was its bucolic, picturesque setting. Most of the orchards had little irrigation rivulets that ran around the contours of the steep hills bringing ice-cold runoff from the slopes of Mt. Hood some thirty miles to our south. When my father was in the precipitous areas of these giants and we had to wait for his return to earth we would seek out the RC Colas and Dad's Root Beer that we had deposited in little reservoirs we would build in the little brooks. We would take our working boots off, stick our feet in for as long as we could stand the cold and slam a few cold ones thinking that it 'Don't get no better than this' moment.

There were a few times when the Oregon harvest would end a bit prematurely and the Washington harvest would be late. Never one to let a good summer day go by without picking something, my dad would always find some form of picking to fill in the gap. We harvested strawberries, hops and 'blackcaps,' which were black raspberries with thorns on steroids.

One such blackcap venue took place in McMinnville, Oregon. When we arrived there, the landowner had no place for us to live, but offered a retired chicken coop as an alternative. My mother really put her foot down on that one and refused to stay in the coop. We spent almost two weeks picking the black fruit and lived at a campground, sleeping on the car rooftop hotel on four wheels. We did spend one night in a motel when we finished before heading off to Wenatchee. After two weeks of picking blackcaps, we all had many thorn pokes, raw sore hands, and beleaguered backs. Fortunately, that was our only foray into that type of harvest.

Chapter Sixteen

"Just know you're not alone
Cause I'm going to make this place your home."
Phillip Phillips
Home

Venue number three was in Wenatchee, Washington in a place called Wenatchee Heights. To call this the armpit of our various incarcerations would make it difficult to assign other odious body sites with names that matched the other abodes. This place screamed for the help of unions and county sanitation intervention.

The geography of this area lacked the sub alpine feel of both The Dalles and Hood River locations. It was essentially a combination of arid, desert land mixed in with vast wheat fields that were dry and amber ready for harvest.

The Wenatchee Heights area was an elevated plateau of several square miles consisting of extensive orchards mixed with cholla and other species of cactus and dried out sage.

Our home away from home was an abandoned ranch house that could have passed for the movie setting of the house in Psycho. It had once been an elegant mansion, but had fallen on hard times. The house was easily two thousand square feet in size, had no electricity or running water. With no other possible accommodations within some 20 miles, we had to make do with this place.

My mom, bless her weary soul, somehow made it work by commandeering large sections of canvass that she used to cordon off a manageable amount of living space. With some of the scrap lumber that was within and without the property we built a table-like structure to accommodate the Coleman and a washbasin that had the duplicitous task of providing a place to wash dishes, clothing, and bodies.

The source of water was a spring a little short of a mile down a rocky path that we shared with an occasional rattlesnake. We slept on air mattresses on top of our canvass flooring and had a makeshift barrier to keep the snakes from entering the doorless entryway.

My siblings and I were the water bearers. Three of us would take two five gallon pails and the fourth would lead the way with a worry stick to make sure that our path was snake free. The trip back was a challenge, as we had to negotiate and ascend the steep trail back to our house. To this day when I'm standing in a hot shower I'll occasionally reflect on the cold water sponge baths that I took in that miserable old house.

Chapter Seventeen

Beyond our June indenture and the relatively familiar but Spartan accommodations at the Pinks, the balance of our summer was always an escapade and a test of my mother's fortitude. The upside was that we were seeing new parts of the Northwest, meeting new people, finding new churches, and seeking out some temporary hovel to call home for a few weeks. Some were in beautiful places, others were oppressive and incarceratous.

Working for the Tamura brothers in the Hood River area was a bit of both. We actually found an abode in the small hamlet of Odell, population 235. Many of the western cities through which we traveled posted the cities' name and head count as you entered its boundary. The first visual impression usually validated the tally displayed on the sign.

The geography of Odell was picturesque but the city structures were run down and dilapidated. We found our way to a cinder block structure with an architecturally cell-like, third rate-romance motel look to it that consisted of a long row of indistinguishable units differing only by door numbers. Each 150 square foot cell block was embellished with two or three beds, a sink, toilet, and no windows. We hauled in our Coleman stove, a folding camp table that my dad had made for such circumstances, added the ubiquitous cherry box chairs and the multi-purpose, one room hut now had its kitchen. On a return visit years later I discovered that the building had been used as an internment center for Japanese POWs during WWII, likely incarcerating many of the locals who were now orchard owners and our bosses.

Odell had little in the way of diversion in the unlikely event that we would ever divert. It did however have a swimming hole in which we occasionally cooled our heels. It had a wooden platform floating near the middle and a large dead tree that had managed to find a watery grave on one side. The water always had a healthy algae bloom that formed a blanket of blue green scum over some of the pond, especially near the dead tree. We helped the locals keep a swimming area clear simply by all of our flailing bodies breaking up the slick and pushing it away from the raft and the entry area. The locals had dubbed it as 'polio pond' but we all managed to avoid the iron-lung disease that had the nation pretty freaked out in the 50's and 60's. The upside of Odell was its proliferation of fruit stands that would take local fruit varieties and blend them along with ice cream into outrageous concoctions. It didn't require much imagination or cash to find a diversion that interceded in the mundane task of picking fruit from daybreak till late afternoon on sultry summer days. Pulling up to one of the ubiquitous roadside stands and ordering a fresh black raspberry or strawberry/cherry shake was right up there with Jack's Hamburgers, six for a dollar burgers, and attempts at going to a drive-in movie where all of us would be asleep in the '49 Chevy before the movies' plot was uncovered.

The late '40s music was dominated by crooners like Frank Sinatra, Bing Crosby, Patsy Cline, Rosemary Clooney, Perry Como and the Dorsey brothers. I shudder to think about my parent's reaction to the music of today, especially if they could observe the adornment of video escapades while listening. I hate rap style music. My parents likely roll in their grave if there is such a thing as a music feed in caskets. They would likely have after death coronaries if they could watch a Super Bowl halftime show. Around 1950, the transistor radio appeared on the electronic scene along with the advent of Rock and Roll. Life in the orchard took a huge turn to the upside with my Cracker Jack box-sized radio complete with a jack for a headphone. In spite of my father's declaration of the satanic nature of Elvis, Chubby Checkers, Deon and his Belmonts, and others, the tinny sound of my little radio beating out its rhythmic sound waves helped us through the drudgery of our labors. The radio also saved me from being a total 'what's cool in music' geek when I returned home the day before school resumed. Each fall on my return to school I had to deal with the rebukes from my classmates calling me a cherry, a cherry picker or fruit tramp.

As our summer sojourns continued I went from elementary, to middle school and then on to high school. The recriminations and embarrassment for the first few weeks of school became increasingly difficult for me. It may not have been as bad as I had perceived it to be, but when I started chasing girls in earnest it was difficult to explain my summer absence and somehow try to avoid revealing that we were migrant laborers.

The level of discomfort that I experienced paled radically in comparison to things that my grandchildren share with me about their school experiences, even though they appear to be quite normal, at least to me.

Chapter Eighteen

Sometime during the late summer prior to my entering the sixth grade my father made his annual phone call to the school district where he taught, to acquire the information for the coming year—the start date, his class schedule and his raise if any were proffered. His previous year's salary, 1953, was $5,400. So, our summer earnings were fairly essential to making those proverbial, elusive ends meet. He returned from that journey into Bigfork, Montana, the nearest home of a pay phone booth with somber and foreboding body language, giving us all reason to think that someone had died in our family.

The grief and anxiety that he expressed was a reaction to the news that he had been fired from his teaching job. A subsequent phone call to the principal and then the superintendent shed no light as to the reasons for his dismissal. In an earlier chapter I alluded to the class structure of Denison, and his suspicion that the reasons for the termination were likely a result of that culture. His replacement was the antithesis of my father; a golfer, socialite and member of the town's country club. My father, who unlike me, was relatively passive and compliant, pretty much let the loss of his teaching job pass as a '*que sera sera*.' Without the benefit of the NEA teacher's union, or much social connectedness he became an unemployed ex teacher. The upshot of this news was pretty devastating to our family who would be facing a fall return to our home with no job, no income and little that could be done to ameliorate the situation between the time of receiving the news and the start of school. In those days, communication was bereft of internet searches, iPhone correspondence and exacerbated by the reality of the nearest pay phone some 10 miles down a dusty road.

We turned to the only solution that made any sense under the circumstances; we decided to continue on as migrants into the fall apple season by returning to Washington state. The cherry harvest on the East Lake Shore of Flathead Lake usually ended in late August giving us about a week or two to seek out employment in the fall apple harvest. Our fruit tramp friends were a good resource for finding housing and employment, 'housing' being a subjective noun as we would soon discover.

Following the Flathead Lake harvest season, we spent our two or three-day interlude being tourists. It's been too many years to remember exactly where or what attraction we might have visited, but we likely ventured into Glacier National Park in northern Montana. If there was such a thing as a list of the top 100 tourist attractions in the western United States, my guess is that we had visited all of them over the dozen or so summers of my discontent. My dad was also enamored with Bureau of Land Management dam projects so we always had to visit one of the most recently completed behemoths added to the water drainages of the arid west. I thought the dams all looked pretty much the same, but I was intrigued by the lame attempts of the engineers to mitigate the damages of blocking the migratory paths of spawning salmon.

Following our brief respite in the glorious environs of Glacier and likely visit to Grand Coulee dam we ended up literally at the end of the world, at least the end of the Northwestern US in a place called Manson, Washington. Manson was the very last outpost on state highway 150 where the pavement ended at the wilderness separating the US and Canada. It was early September, and I longed to go home. As far as I could discern, I may as well have been in a Siberian prison camp.

Our first order of business was to enroll in the local school system. I ended up in the sixth grade class taught by a sadistic, imposing hulk of a man, Patrick Bagloff. Up to this point in my educational journey I was generally a good student, with good marks in most courses though fluctuating marks in the citizenship (behavior) column commensurate with the symbiosis with the teacher. In kindergarten and second grade I was in love with my teachers so those attitude marks were good.

I was not in love with Mr. Bagloff. There were 15 or so in my grade level made up mostly of orchard owner's children and a handful of migrant kids whose parents worked for them. Mr. Bagloff had a hard on for the fruit tramp kids, all of whom happened to be males. He would exclude us from participating in the classroom and would insult us if we answered incorrectly or made a mistake.

During a recess early in the year he called me and four of my migrant peers into his office where he proceeded to force us to drop our pants and shorts and gave us each a whack with a paddle. And, yes it had holes drilled through the surface. The uncivil act of abuse caused a bond to develop among our group and we steeled ourselves to similar attacks throughout the fall term.

One evening when getting ready for bed, my dad noticed that my butt was black and blue and wanted to know what had happened to me. When I told him that I didn't really know why I had been smacked with the paddle he responded as only a wary father and himself a teacher could. He assumed that I had it coming to me and told me that I would get a double dose of the same discipline at home if he verified what he supposed to be true.

He made an appointment with the teacher, the principal and towed me along to this assemblage. I was pretty ambivalent and most of all didn't want to be in the presence of Mr. Bagloff. My dad asked the teacher to explain what I had done to earn my punishment. He said that I had been unruly and had caused problems to others on the playground and that I hung around with a group of other boys who were troublemakers. My dad pressed on for specifics and when none were verbalized, the principal asked for my version of the events. I commented that the five of us were all migrant fruit pickers and the only boys from the class who had been disciplined.

When it became apparent that the only physical punishment was being meted out to the migrant boys, my father went somewhat ballistic with the teacher and asked the principal to expound on the *in loco parentis* laws of the state of Washington. I have very sweet memories of that moment. The principal and teacher were instantly alert and aware that they weren't dealing with some fruit bum, but a well-educated and legally informed father who had just witnessed a serious discrimination and abuse event. Following some legal threats by my father we ended our little visit with assurances and ass kissings from both men promising that further such incidents would likely never happen again.

We stayed in Manson for the balance of the apple harvest and completed the fall term without further incidents, but the seeds of discontent and my perception of my academic aptitude would suffer a blow that would drag me down throughout my secondary and into the early years of my college educational experience. It took me many years to finally figure out that I could be a good student and that I was actually pretty smart.

My educational odyssey was interrupted several years later when I flunked out after my first two years of college. A few years later I finally ventured back to the University of Colorado, with the help of a wonderful Journalism dean, Dean Brinton, who along with a couple of wonderful and encouraging professors got me on the right academic track culminating with a degree in journalism.

In the lifeline of most young people, the rear view mirror on life sheds its beam on a handful of people, either intent on mentoring or just being good people that crossed one's path. I certainly was blessed at those junctures in life when those people became lifesavers and page turners. As a believer, I know that one day I will again cross paths with them and will shower them with accolades of thanksgiving and grace.

Chapter Nineteen

"When you think you're at the end of the road,
Let go and let God share your load,
Your work is not finished or ended,
You've just come to a bend in the road."
Helen Steiner Rice
The End of the Road is But a Bend in the Road

Manson was a small town of some 600 hundred local residents, mostly orchard owners and a few merchants. Even though it was isolated from the world, it was located on Lake Chelan and had a very nice swimming area that we would visit almost daily after school and on weekends. The swimming area consisted of a large deck adjacent to the beach with a large roped off swimming area to keep children from venturing out into Lake Chelan that was large enough (100 plus miles in length and several miles wide) to have a leviathan monster. We enjoyed the swimming hole very much but by mid-October, the fall temperatures ended that attraction.

The apple orchards of that area produce a significant portion of the US and world's apple supply. Like all orchard environments in the '40s and '50s, they were reliant on migrant labor to complete the harvest. And, like all harvest environments not much was dedicated to housing for the three-month harvest season.

We worked for a large agricultural complex that owned a few thousand acres of Delicious, Golden Delicious, and other varieties. Apple picking was quite different from cherries but utilized similar ladders to access the fruit. For cherry picking we wore a harness that supported a galvanized 30-quart pail that carried the fruit. Apple pickers wore a similar harness but it was outfitted with a large rimmed canvas bag that was open at the bottom but sequestered with ropes on each side that were pulled up and latched to keep the apples in place until the container was full.

When full, the picker would lean down over a wood crate that would hold roughly a bushel of apples, release the ropes, and carefully allow the apples to tumble from the bag to the box. Care had to be taken to avoid bruising as the apples tumbled down into the box. A full apple bag was much heavier than a cherry pail and the work was physically more challenging as the picker would negotiate down a ladder with a full bag that could easily weigh 50 pounds.

And, like cherry trees, apple trees were often homes to hornet nests, attracting the pests by providing them with a camouflaged and safe home surrounded by good things to eat. It was not unusual for a picker to reach for a spur of cherries or apples, only to grab a hornet's nest causing a minor catastrophe when angry hornets would look for any open flesh on a fruit picker's body while they were trying to hang on to a ladder several feet in the air.

Our four-month temporary home in Manson consisted of a one-room 350 square foot hut with outside plumbing and relieving. We did have one electric light bulb hanging from the rafter and one outlet that we used to feed an electric heater when the chilly weather invaded our abode in the fall and early winter months.

There was a communal unisex shower facility that required a family member to guard the entrance hopefully avoiding any surprise visits by the opposite sex. It had two shower heads, so two could bathe at once and it was always a race to get there before the hot water was gone.

Our cabin was two miles from school, so we walked to school every day and were released at two in the afternoon, so that we could join our parents to pick apples until five o'clock or so in the afternoon. Oftentimes our financial situation would provide a lean lunch so taking one big Red Delicious apple in our lunch pail would supplement our noonday meal. Some of the apples were large enough to feed three people, and after far too many meals of apples I don't have much of a hankering for eating them to this day.

Chapter Twenty

"School days, school days,
Good old golden rules days
Readin' 'ritin' and 'rithmetic
Taught to the tune of the hickory stick"
Will Cobb/Gus Edwards
School Days

In late December 1953 following the apple harvest and travails of our migrant experience in Manson we hopped in the old Chevy and headed for the already harvested cornfields of Iowa and home. We made it before Christmas and enjoyed a few weeks of respite away from the strange environment and the anthropology of being fruit pickers.

I rejoined my Denison classmates after a seven-month absence and felt much like I had felt in my class in Manson—an outsider and uncomfortable. My sixth grade teacher, Helen Stengel (the strangler) saddled me with the label of being 'incorrigible,' and I received very poor marks for citizenship, joining the low marks of my other subjects. In retrospect I can verbalize and understand the mechanics of what I was trying to accomplish with my unruly behavior. I felt out of place and inferior and I had a great need to draw attention to myself by attempting to be the class clown. I was pretty funny to most of my classmates, but not so amusing to the strangler. My grades were awful and I failed in the citizenship category. I started believing that I was not very smart and my grades reflected that conviction.

I bonded with other malcontent students and disdained those in my class who were the 'brains.' I still have all of my old report cards and the stark comparison of my marks in grades K-5 and 6-12 and early college reflect the radical transition that my scholastic psyche had suffered thanks to my experience under Mr. Bagloff's tutelage. At the date of this writing if he is still alive, he would likely be at least in his mid-90's. If he happens to read this, he is welcome to sue me for defamation.

I did survive the 6th grade, but barely. I hung on to the few things that I was good at doing, providing just enough self-esteem to get me through. I was good in P.E. and always won the classroom games of eraser tag and came in first or second in all of the spelling bees, either winning or coming in second to Karen Mullenger.

My father was never re-hired as a teacher and found employment through the grace of Dick Knowles who owned the *Denison Bulletin and Review* newspaper. My dad traveled the extent of Crawford County selling subscriptions to the paper and became a 'stringer' for the paper, writing a newsy column about the rural inhabitants of Crawford County, their births, anniversaries, weddings, excursions and deaths.

One of the side perks of his visit to the farms led to a growing interest in antiques, mostly lamps. While visiting rural homesteads he would always inquire about the availability of any antique lamps the occupants might possess. More often than not he

would come up with antique lamps that had been relegated to the attic or basement with the advent of electric lights in the late '30s and early '40s. Over the next six or seven years he collected several hundred lamps, getting many of them for 'a song.' He restored all of the lamps, some with a value into the hundreds of dollars. He had a great mechanical aptitude for woodworking and restoration and electrified many of the lamps maintaining their authenticity, yet giving them a practical life as an antique lighting fixture. Several are still adorning our home and the homes of my siblings and their children. One double globe painted beauty assists in lighting the area at this very writing workstation.

My dad's income along with my mom's part-time salary as a Hested Lee clerk provided enough to get us through the school year. My siblings and I were allowed to keep most of our summer earnings, so in spite of living in a not-so-well-to-do family, I always had spending money and even opened my own bank account when I was eleven. I was the envy of my cash poor friends, but they likely wouldn't consider trading places in the summertime.

The good news was that my dad had pretty much decided to end his teaching career avoiding a move to another town, and was content to languish away his considerable skills by staying with the *Denison Bulletin and Review*.

My father grew up in northern Iowa, the son of a banker, was a good student and aspired to becoming a doctor. He was an athlete and involved in a number of extracurricular activities. His love of sports carried over into his teaching career and he was the varsity basketball coach in his first teaching assignment.

His teams were very successful, with annual visits to the state basketball tournament, ending up a few times in the final four of Class A sized high schools, the smallest at the time in the state of Iowa. In the fall of 1939 he moved his family consisting then of his wife and one daughter to Denison, Iowa, three years before I joined the world. It has always amazed me how one's anthropology is so indiscriminate and so dependent on things so far beyond one's control. My father, an aspiring medical practitioner, ended up as a part-time migrant laborer all the result of a nation's disastrous financial crisis and his parent's vocation and DNA. In modern times our situation would likely result in receiving government support through the welfare system. That would never have been the path that my father would have pursued, nor any of his offspring.

Chapter Twenty-One

"Feeling tired and weary from my head
To my shoes
I got a low down feeling, truck driver's blues."
Ferlin Husky
Truck Driver Blues

Though our fall apple picking adventure never happened again, we continued our cherry picking routine without interruption for the next six years. In 1960 my family moved from Iowa to Colorado and my parents both got decent jobs. I continued on with the summer harvest routine a few years into my early college epoch.

In the summer of 1955, my first year as a teenager, Dave Pink, the orchard owner and his foreman, Gilbert Benson offered me a job as a 'swamper.' I was all of five foot four and a strapping 120 pounds. Instead of picking cherries along with the rest of my family I learned to drive a Dodge Power Wagon towing a large flatbed trailer. Along with the orchard foreman and Dave, I would drive the truck on the contours of the hilly countryside to the areas of the orchard that were being harvested. We would approach trees that had just been harvested and would weigh each box and credit the picker who was identified by a tag with their personal number. Dave's wife, Barbara would often ride along to be the recorder of the weighing process.

My job was to drive the truck to a location of a finished harvested tree, identify the picker by their card inserted number. Each box was then lifted to the flatbed of the trailer and stacked in such a manner to compensate for the slope of the part of the orchard where we happened to be. The process would go on until the flat bed had seven boxes across, four or five high and fifteen deep, some 300 crates weighing around 15,000 pounds. I would then drive the load back to the packing shed taking great care to not violate the laws of physics and gravity precariously keeping my load right side up. Amazingly, I never had one mishap and never dumped a load.

When I first learned to drive the truck, well before driving age, I could barely depress the clutch to shift properly, so I started the job with great anxiety and a feeling of incompetence. The job didn't require much cerebral input, but was physically very demanding. Along with my father I questioned my ability to survive the rigorous demands of the job, but the $100 per-day pay scale enticed me to give it a go.

During the course of a 12-hour day, I would lift each crate to be weighed, lift it from the scale to the flat bed, and transfer it from the flatbed to a large semi-trailer handling each crate three times. The process was repeated throughout the day until all boxes were picked up, weighed, and sent to a packing plant in The Dalles at mid-day and again at the end of the day often totaling some 40 tons of harvested cherries each day of the season.

The orchard was large and the distance from top to bottom was more than a half mile and two miles from the outer tree rows to the packing shed. As sections and species of the orchard were completed, I would also drive the truck to that area and stack all of the ladders used in the harvest, load up the harvesters and haul them together to the next segment to be picked. The orchards were void of any ground cover and were tilled topsoil that purposely was very dry. By the end of the day any exposed skin, my face, hands, eyeballs, and ears were laden with grit.

After transferring the last crates to the semi, my job was to service the truck that seemed to leak engine oil and axle grease profusely. I was usually done by six o'clock as well as being 'done in,' the last of all the workers to take a shower in our solar-powered water heating system. I would barely make it to our canvass walled partition in time for dinner and rarely could stay awake beyond 7 o'clock.

I survived that first summer and took a certain amount of pride in the completion of a very physically demanding job. I became pretty ripp with very calloused and muscled hands. And quite wealthy for a young teen boy in the 50's earning around three thousand dollars for the Pink's harvest.

Chapter Twenty-Two

The end of each harvest was gloriously welcomed, but at the same time a sad event. Our family would bond with a number of the perennial returnees and each family unit would venture off to another job venue and rarely did we see any of those Oregon people at the places we moved on to.

The glorious part was on the day following harvest completion, all of the pickers would be scrubbed and dressed in the clothing that differed from the work duds that adorned us for a month or so. The owner would provide a watermelon and ice cream fest and we would gather in a grassy shaded part of the owner's backyard and have a feast and fellowship. For the first time we would wear shorts and dresses for the most part exposing ghastly white skin with inordinately darker skin on our hands, faces and necks.

The 'slopping up' was the grand finale. Dave Pink would have made a trip to the bank for the huge amounts of cash he needed to settle all of the accounts.

He would present us with a record of each day's production and the cumulative total for each day of the harvest that we would compare against our own tallies. The total tonnage was multiplied by the going harvest rate and each picker would step up to the table to receive our wad of cash.

My family would usually end up with a sum in excess of three thousand dollars, which was more than half of my father's annual teacher's salary.

As a swamper I would almost equal the earned sum of my entire family. In retrospect I felt like the richest kid on earth and probably was for a teenager in the 1950's. Upon reflection of those years I resented how hard I worked for that money and what I gave up by never experiencing a summer that a normal child got to enjoy. For my childhood, there was never summer.

The rest of the day was spent re packing our various modes of transportation and saying our goodbyes. Most families had old, dilapidated pickups before the days of crew cabs. They would load up the back end, then parlay for a ride in the cab with the losers jammed in the rear with all of the gear. I was always amazed at the sadness that I experienced when this separation took place. The work was so hard that camaraderie would naturally develop much like soldiers in a foxhole. We also lived with just the thickness of canvass separating our lives, so our secrets were few and we knew more about each other than we cared to know.

Walking through the empty packing shed imparted a lonesome feeling, the progeny of the absence of the sounds and smells of close-quarter habitation. That was always a sad experience and would immediately invoke sentiments of looking forward to the next harvest season.

The latter season venues in Washington and Montana had much smaller orchards, smaller crews and scattered living quarters that didn't impart the same sociological aspects that an eclectic group of some 40 people generated. My sibling sisters and I have cogitated many times about how much we loathed the dreariness of our summer labors, but also how profound and somewhat treasured are the memories of those lost summer months of our childhood. The four of us have grown children and grandchildren and we rarely are under the same roof at the same time. When we have the luxury of such a gathering there is a noticeable dissonance of many voices and the chaos of little people's actions intruding on our concerted efforts to converse. But, we will infrequently be raconteurs of those summer months and always find the recollections to be humorous and bawdy and rarely a commiseration of those summer less days.

Chapter Twenty-Three

"Oh Montana, give this child a home
Give him the love of a good family and a woman of
his own
Give him a fire in his heart, give him a light in his
eyes
Give him the wild wind for a brother and the wild
Montana skies."
John Denver
Wild Montana Skies

The extent of our summers from Memorial Day through Labor Day, save for the one extended year for the apple harvest, always consumed the entire three-month summer absence from school. Unlike the school calendar today we had the luxury of a full three months without school that has been so radically shortened, starting now usually in mid-August.

Our third venue of the typical summer was one that we almost looked forward to, arriving in the sub alpine geography of the East Flathead Lake area of northwestern Montana.

Flathead Lake is one of the largest freshwater lakes in North America, some 40 plus miles in length and 15 miles wide at its waistline. The lake is gin clear and the bottom is visible up to 50 feet in depth on a calm day.

The riparian area of the East Lake Shore from its southern tip in Polson 35 miles north to Bigfork consisted of hundreds of cherry orchards on both sides of Highway 35, some extending almost to the shores of Flathead on the west side of the highway and up and into the foothills of the Flathead Mountain Range and the Bob Marshall Wilderness area east of the highway. The orchards were numerous and small, interspersed with forested areas and unlike the orchards of Oregon and Washington had grassy ground cover providing a more user-friendly landscape, almost a picnic like, bucolic setting. Eating our lunches on the verdant mixture of grass and weeds whilst looking through the pines at intervocalic glimpses of the lake sure beat the dusty hillsides of our previous jobs.

The numerous orchards of the area ranged in size from a couple of acres to as large as a hundred acres. It was a challenge to find enough growers to keep us busy for the duration of harvest. The geography and climate of western Montana dictated an erratic pattern of harvest ripeness for the owners and we would work for as many as a dozen different orchards, often moving from one to the other almost daily to meet the demands of harvest readiness.

Our choice of accommodations consisted of a few cheap motels that catered to the tourists that heavily traveled that area in August. Our budget pretty much ruled out that option, so we lived in our car top camper in one of the campgrounds on the shore of the lake. We camped either at Yellow Bay or Woods Bay and could at least enjoy the esoteric of camping, by pretending that we were tourists, complete with a campfire and lake fishing, but out of there at daybreak leaving our tourism to pursue our agrarian tasks.

My dad, of course, found the nearest church, The Congregational Church in Bigfork, a town in those days of some 700 full time residents. The small town boomed to several thousand seasonal visitors including a fair number of fruit tramps. Dad made an acquaintance with several good church folks, particularly a couple who were elderly and very involved with the church.

Harry and Connie Lay, a couple in their mid-70's owned an orchard some ten miles to the south of Bigfork. They were intrigued by the inimitable spirit of our family and the anomalies that we displayed in contrast to the typical migrant groups. They hired us to pick their orchard and when they discovered that we were living in our car, they offered us accommodations in a two-bedroom log cabin on their property.

When we first arrived we discovered a two-acre orchard that we could harvest in one or two days and our hope for our own cabin in the woods soon dissipated, realizing that we could complete Harry's orchard in one good day. They were such gracious people and offered the cabin for the entire length of our stay in Montana whether working their orchard or not.

It was glorious, complete with two bathrooms, hot and cold running water, a gas stove with an oven and a refrigerator. There was a small, one-foot wide spring-fed creek that drained the snow melt from the mountain range to the east that trickled right through our grassy yard and near enough to our bedroom windows to provide the luscious melody of cascading water.

We each had our own beds although a shared bedroom. On days that we would return late from another orchard, Connie would invite our family to their house for dinner providing us with a rare, complete three course meal.

When it was time to harvest Harry's orchard, Harry would sound like an orchard owner with hundreds of acres. He would fuss about our starting too early in the morning and stress about the harvested cherries if we stacked the crates in the sun. He would make a comment like, "I think in a few hours we'll be right in the middle of it," meaning the midpoint of the harvest. During the fifth or so year working for the Lays, Harry was excited to find that I had 'swamper' experience which would lessen his burden of getting the fruit to market. When we finished his orchard on the same day, he was always amazed that we were so efficient and would lavish praise on us.

We felt somewhat guilty that we occupied his cabin when we only worked for him one or two days. My dad took the culpability rather seriously, offering my services to help Harry with other chores around the place when our day was finished. I would chop and stack firewood, prune his cherry trees, mow the grass, and work wherever else he needed help.

We would usually end our day around 5 p.m. and when I didn't have my cabin thanksgiving duties, the four of us would trudge down a very steep road to the lake for a swim. The sun in August was still producing solar energy in the late afternoon and would take some of the sting from our bodies after a plunge in the 65-degree water of Flathead. Harry had a supply of inner tubes and other floating devices on his shore front, so we would swim until the gonies and skin shriveled and were completely laden with goose bumps. That small touch of summer recreation was just enough to remind us that we were almost like other children pursuing the delights of summer.

I was also an avid fisherman and would spend as much of my free time as possible casting lures to the cutthroat trout of the lake and in the nearby Swan River. I inadvertently learned the rudiments of fly fishing when I discovered that putting a live Hellgrammite on a bare hook and floating it into an eddy or a pocket below a large boulder would most often yield a nice, fat trout. Any of our recreational forays were always followed by the completion of a 10 or 11-hour day, so I wasn't exactly the 'barefoot boy with cheeks of tan, kissed by strawberries on the hill," born of the pen of John Greenleaf Whittier.

When we first arrived in Montana in the summer of 1950 we had just worked for a month each in Oregon and Washington spending almost the entire month in each state in one large orchard. So, the prospect of lining up several orchards and orchestrating the timing of the ripening fruit was a new challenge. We would literally drive from one driveway to the next inquiring about the prospects of harvesting their crop.

Over the course of the next decade we managed to work for some of the same owners each year while staying at the cabin. Most of the owners were nice people with full-time occupations elsewhere, who would spend a week or two attending to the obligations of the harvest. Often we would be the only pickers hired as the needs of the small orchards called for fewer laborers to complete the job.

One such orchard family, the Ossloffs, were looking for more people for their harvest. We drove to their place and my dad went up to the home to inquire about their harvest needs. Mrs. Ossloff came out to our car and spoke with my mom while my dad was negotiating with her husband. She was obviously a bit taken aback when she saw the five of us in the car and asked about our accommodations. She yelled back to one of her children near the house and told her to bring us some fresh water and to make sure to bring drinking cups, the ones without a handle. Our impression of the Ossloff's was obviously not one of affection or fondness and for some reason, we did not get the job.

Me and my siblings were all pretty astute and clearly felt the sting of their disdain.

We verbally conjured up some pranks of retribution that we never pursued, but one in particular we still talk about in amusement to this day. Our plan was to share a paper grocery bag for a temporary latrine, in the dark of night, take it and its contents to their doorstep, light it on fire, ring the doorbell and run like hell. Hell hath no fury like a mistaken identity of a middle class family being confused for migrant white trash. On many occasions since, when we are together and discussing unpleasant people and having a few laughs, it is likely that one of us will make a well-used statement, "poop on Ossloffs." It always elicits a laugh and a shared memory.

Another such orchard owner was the Uren family who owned an orchard on the lake side of highway 93. Mr. Uren had a significant jewelry business in Calgary and the orchard and lake front property were a late summertime hobby. During the time of the harvest on their land, I became acquainted with their son, John, who was my age. Our family plans that August were to move from Denison, Iowa, to Boulder, Colorado. When he heard this, he was elated because he had planned on matriculating at the University of Colorado the following year.

He eventually came to CU and we became fast friends. We had many good times. Both of us being very competitive, we had many sports contests; skiing, cross country skiing, badminton, and wrestling. We have stayed in touch over the many years and are on each other's Christmas list. He is a pure and unapologetic Canuck and still claims that Canada has better hockey and that the Canadian Rockies are higher than the Colorado Rockies. You can google that, John, for the real truth.

At times we would split the family and accommodate the needs of two orchards at a time. There were many times when we would be without any work if the ripening timing was off. It didn't take my father long to squelch any of our dreams of enjoying leisure time. There were a number of fresh fruit stands adjacent to the East Lake Shore highway laden with summer tourists, many traveling there for the sole purpose of buying fresh fruit. The Lays owned such a stand in front of their property and it had gone unused for a number of years. They allowed us to place some signs along the highway in both directions announcing the offering of our produce in our new-found occupation.

A number of the orchards advertised a 'U-Pick' feature that would allow customers to pick their own fruit at a much-reduced cost per pound, usually 10 to 15 cents per pound. On our off-days five of us would go and pick several hundred pounds, while my father would occupy the fruit stand, selling our gleanings for 50 to 75 cents per pound depending on the variety of cherry. My dad was a crafty marketer and learned rather quickly to provide different types of containers that would contain three, five and ten pound quantities offering a volume discount to the purchaser. On a good weekend day, he could garner several hundreds of dollars from our efforts.

The rest of us would have a shortened day harvesting and the automobile traffic would be pretty much gone by late afternoon. A few really short days allowed time for us to live it up by driving some 40 miles north to Kalispell, go out to dinner and if we could stay awake, go to a movie. I still have mostly good memories of our times at Flathead Lake. Sometimes if we arrived at Flathead too early for the

harvest or had a few spare days before heading home we would splurge and head a short distance north and cruise through Glacier National Park, or travel good back roads and pick huckleberries. The berries were always in very remote and mountainous areas and we would see much wildlife; bear, deer, elk, badgers and an occasional moose. On one such outing, we were on a very rugged mountain road and while picking huckleberries, we heard some loud crashing noises coming from the brushy areas near the road. Soon, a moose appeared and we climbed into our car. There was a large road grader nearby and the moose wasn't too happy about its intrusion. He pawed the dirt a few times in front of the behemoth and proceeded to crash into it with its massive antlers. After a few unsuccessful attempts, he sauntered back into the woods, likely licking his parts.

Chapter Twenty-Four

"Clear eyes
Full hearts
Can't lose."
Friday Nights' motto

The Montana cherry season usually shuts down near the end of August. We rarely had more than a week to pack our stuff into the old Chevy and head for Iowa, some four states and 1700 miles away. We almost always went back through Yellowstone National Park on our journey back home.

We enjoyed the luxury of spending a day and night in one of the log cabins at Fishing Bridge in Yellowstone. We would rent a small fishing boat and go trolling for trout on Yellowstone Lake, almost always catching a limit that we would clean, put on ice

for the trip home, and save some for a fish feed in our cabin. We would fry them on the surface of the pot-bellied stove that adorned each cabin, providing a source of heat and the culinary needs of the frying pan.

In the fifties and sixties, the bear population in Yellowstone was significant. It was not uncommon to have 'bear jams' on the highways when a bruin would cross the highway. They were frequent visitors to campgrounds and cabin areas and a general nuisance to park visitors and to the Park Rangers. I could tell a number of bear related stories, but will share just a few. Once when camping, our next door camper-neighbor, had just caught a number of fish and had cleaned them, put them in an ice filled, state of the art new metal Coleman cooler. My dad politely suggested to the man that he put the cooler in the trunk of his car, but the man explained that the new metal coolers, with slide over bars to the top were bomb and bear proof. We had just climbed into our roof top camper when out on the lawn there arose such a clatter. We all watched with the aid of my father's flashlight as the bear easily ripped the cover of the cooler off and ate the fish before moving on to the next feast.

On another occasion we had rented a boat at the mouth of the Yellowstone River at the Fishing Bridge boat rental and marina. We had been out fishing for two or three hours and were returning to the marina. There is a large gravel bar on the east side of the river before you pass under the Fishing Bridge. It is barren with just a few trees and a lot of people venture out there to fish and to hike. When we approached the mouth of the river a large crowd had gathered and there was a lot of commotion. Apparently, a bear had also ventured into the area and over-friendly tourists had ticked off the bear. He proceeded to harass some of the people and eventually treed a young boy. The boy had climbed up the tree as far as he could go without breaking off the top branches, his only exit route. The bear was big enough and wise enough to know that he also could go no further up the tree. The standoff lasted for almost an hour before the Park Rangers arrived. They cleared the area of all but the kid's family and tried to goad the animal to retreat without success. The sad ending came when the ranger had to shoot the bear, all visible to us from our parked boat.

Somewhere in my photo archives, I have pictures of many of those events, but like most Americans, they know they have them but can't find them.

We would usually leave Montana with a large quantity of fresh cherries that we consumed along the way. My mother would use the major portion of the cherries for canning. We would spend a lot of time pitting them before she would cook them on the stove in the Yellowstone cabin and then put them in jars. I'm not sure and can't remember how we managed to get a cooler with fish and four or five cases of canned cherries to fit in the already overloaded Chevy, but my father had an uncanny knack for squeezing it all in.

Needless to say, the trip from Montana to Iowa was painstakingly slow with four weary siblings anxious to get home and renew friendships. By the end of summer we had exhausted our supply of comic books, so we relied on games to help ease the monotony of 50 mile-per-hour, two-lane highway, four day trips. We would make up games along the way, like seeing who could count the most windmills. We knew the shape and design of all of the cars on the road and what every state's license plate looked like. By the time we had endured half of Nebraska, we would enter the humidity zone so prevalent in the Midwest.

The weather in late august in Iowa was still very hot and humid and local folks claimed that on a sizzling, muggy night they could actually hear the corn growing. The excitement of nearing home and the radical change of environment had to be contrasted to the lovely climate of Montana with the moderate days and cool nights that made sleeping sublime.

Soon we would be in our non-air-conditioned home and sweating profusely during the day and throughout the night. My parents always made a big deal of that, thinking that it might be some placating for our lost summers telling us how much better we had it by being in places all summer that lacked the humidity. Kids then, just as today have little perception of the nuances of climates and I would have traded months of sweaty days and nights hanging out with my friends for the onus of a tortured summer in the dry heat sweat lodge of a cherry orchard.

Most years we would arrive home a day or two before Labor Day, so we could get a quick dip in the swimming pool before they shut it down. We all looked pretty weird in our swimming togs with lily white skin and baked hands, faces and necks, but it didn't diminish our enthusiasm for a quick shot at enjoying a normal summer day before the advent of school.

I played football, basketball, baseball and ran track and always joined football team practices two weeks late, which didn't exactly endear me to my coaches or give me much hope of playing. Our school baseball season always began in April and extended into the summer. I was a terrific baseball player, but rarely got a chance to play in more than one or two games before the summer season began. I would then have to make my exit when we embarked to places west.

By the time I had entered junior high school, my dad had already lost his teaching job. The social system that I mentioned earlier in my narrative was not really obvious to me as an adolescent, but became more evident as I neared high school. My dad's experience as a coach gave him a pretty good perspective of my athletic abilities. He was well aware of the subtleties of sports competition and the partiality that coaches can so easily apply under the guise of putting the best product on the field.

We had a JV football team that I played on as a freshman and sophomore as a little-used running back. I was still pretty small, maybe five feet five and 125 lbs. I wasn't certain that I really liked football and was probably on the team more because of peer pressure, and the goading from coaches to not be a wimp.

I was a much better basketball player and played some fleeting moments on the varsity as a sophomore when our team was way ahead or way behind. My basketball coach, Jim Matthews was also an assistant football coach and tried as best he could to get playing time for me during the football season. But my dad would jokingly talk about his concern for me, gathering splinters in my butt due to extensive time on the bench.

The football players for the most part were much bigger than me and liked the sport for the chance it provided them to smash someone. A few of the coveted positions were filled by favored guys who were part of the 'in' group and not necessarily as talented as some of us in the 'out' group.

By the start of my junior year I wasn't even sure what position I was supposed to be learning, and got few practice reps at running back. I spent most of the practices holding blocking pads or pushing a sled around. My dad made more out of my lack of notoriety and verbalized what he thought was unfair treatment.

We had only two quarterbacks on the team, a sophomore, Dale Mullen and his back up, Billy Moffett. Dale was a flame throwing baseball pitcher who won most of the games when he pitched, very athletic and the coach's golden boy. Billy was in the same group of businessmen's sons, golfer, clubbie and received favored treatment.

In the early part of the first game of the fall, Dale broke his collarbone, and Billy was sent in to replace him for the rest of the game and the season. He lasted but a few plays and didn't seem to have the warrior's heart necessary to play football. A time out was called as the Denison Monarchs were in a real quandary. Coach Matthews grabbed me and asked me to consider during a three-minute time out to play quarterback. In spite of my lack of practice time I was pretty football savvy and knew all of my assignments as a running back and the interaction with the quarterback.

So, I was sent into the fray. Each called play was sent in via a substitute, who explained which way I was to turn and whom to hand the ball to. Our offense was the famous Winged T designed in the late 50's and early 60's by the University of Iowa head coach, Forrest Evacheski. It was a relatively complex system for high school level football. I survived a few snaps without making a first down but also without a fumble. But, at the very least my feet were wet and we were still in the game.

On our next offensive series, I got confused, turned the wrong direction, and nearly got knocked down by our fullback who hadn't expected me to be running directly at him. I managed to keep my feet on the ground and my hands on the ball and learned the meaning of the words 'scramble' and 'broken play.' I took off in the right direction, avoided any more mishaps with my own players and somehow scored a touchdown. That play was a defining moment and turning point in my life although I hadn't a clue about the significance of its meaning at the time. My father attended all of my games in spite of my inactivity. When some people sitting near him expressed some confusion as to whom the number 28 belonged, my dad proudly stated that it was his son. We tied that game, 7-7

The next week and the weeks following were a serious crash course in learning to quarterback an intricate offense. I wasn't much of a scholar so I dedicated all of my spare time learning the play book, avoiding completely any textbooks.

Our team went on to a six and three record and I grew up in a number of ways, shedding some of the caricatures that I had been saddled with and rinsing my self-images of being a fruit picker, a second stringer and unimportant. I completed over 65 percent of my passes and had over five hundred yards of rushing. I finished the school year as a starting guard on the basketball team, leading the team in scoring, assists and free throw percentage. During my Junior and Senior years playing basketball, I was awarded 132 free throws for being fouled. I made 118. When my dad was coaching, he shared with me an event where he had taken his entire team to a basketball training camp in nearby Des Moines. The camp was led by the legendary coach, Adolf Rupp. If there was one thing that my dad fully retained from that training camp was that Mr. Rupp did not believe in players missing free throws. My dad bought into that edict and through our DNA, it was passed along to me. I still cringe when I watch D1 players or pros step up to the free throw line and miss.

With the arrival of Spring I starred in track as a sprinter and won numerous events. I always ran the 100, 220 and the sprint relays. Our track field was a mile from our high school and we would have to run there and back for each practice day. It was called 'the course.' Everyone hated that part of track practice and I always thought it was kind of like running a marathon. For some strange reason as I aged I was enticed by a friend to sign up for a 10 kilometer race being staged on Memorial Day in Boulder, Colorado, now my home. The first race attracted about 3,000 runners and took place through residential areas of Boulder. As the race grew in ensuing years it eventually attracted over 50,000 runners and the organizers changed the layout of the course ending the race at Folsom Stadium, home to the Colorado Buffaloes football team. So, when one finishes the race they enter the stadium and approach the finish line with some 40 or so thousand people already in the stands to cheer friends or family members. And then, when all the citizen racers are finished everyone stays to watch the professional racers from all over the world race for big prize money. The bank that has organized and sponsored the race now going on 43 years, then holds an incredible Memorial Day celebration with a fly over, veteran salutations and hang gliders floating into the stadium, flying flags representing every branch of service and the penultimate glider descending with the American Flag dropping to the floor of Folsom, while "Proud to Be an American" is played on the stadium sound system.

After 15 years of staging the Bolder Boulder, the bank acknowledged the some 150 people who had run each and every race. They dubbed the group the Boulder Boldest. The group size has shrunk over the years to around 50 or so brave, reverent souls who have completed every single race without fail. I am still a proud member of the Boulder Boldest and completed a few of the races under significant duress; one year after I was in a significant automobile accident, another following bi lateral knee replacement, and a few when I flew all night to return home after attending my daughter's college graduations. Not bad for an athlete who thought that running any distance over 200 yards was cruel and unusual punishment.

During my high school years many years earlier, a written message in my yearbook from coach Matthews made an enormous impact on my self-esteem. He scribed, "Thanks for all of your support in athletics this year. You became a champion and made a man of yourself. Keep up the great work—I'll be watching you. Your coach and friend," ……

I have marveled throughout life how the comments and encouragement of just a few adult mentors can make such an impact on a young mind and orchestrate such a course correction.

Summer came and I had to once again abandon the summer and baseball season to head west, leaving behind my newfound self-esteem. I have been asked if I had ever considered staying with friends for the summer, but I was not comfortable being away from my family and I also felt an obligation to help with family finances.

Chapter Twenty-Five

"When some large bragger tries to put me down
and says his schools is great…"
Beach Boys
Be True to Your School

The summer of 1959 launched our tenth year of fruit tramping. I was nearly 17 and I traded the hours reading comic books and playing marble games for the mind-enriching efforts of visualizing making plays on the football field or scoring the winning basket in a game of hoops. In those days there wasn't much emphasis on year-around training or off-season weightlifting. My swamping chores gave me a one up on my languid, barefoot summer boy teammates by getting me pretty muscled and developing terrific hand strength. I still wasn't very big--five foot, seven and 160 lbs. I had small hands, like my father, but my finger and hand strength was significant with the cherry box lifting and weighing.

I found work crew friends to play catch with at the end of the day, and a few of the orchards had a backboard and hoop, so I would shoot baskets and play catch as long as I could stay awake. That summer seemed to move along a little more quickly and I counted the days until Labor Day.

Our family moved up a bit in status that year with a newer car. The old 1949 Chevy had well over a hundred thousand miles and was pretty well worn out. My dad bought a used 1958, coral and gray Chevy Bel Air that I thought was pretty cool. I was driving by then and like all young men in the 50's, I attached a lot of importance to 'my ride.' It was relatively new, had a four-barrel carburetor and dual exhaust pipes. Relative to most of my friend's family cars, it was pretty fast. I didn't hot rod around in it too much for fear of doing something that might cause damage to my family's most expensive possession aside from our home.

My dad had to spend months before our western  departure to modify our car-top sleeper to fit the new car. I dreaded the thought of being seen by my friends in the car with its tobacco-road likenesses as we headed out of town. I felt that the car topper took away from the good vibes I had gotten from having 'my' new hot car to one of a poor man's camper. I quickly went from the mindset of being the quarterback backward to that of being a water boy and fruit tramp. I felt like I had ventured north across the tracks during that past year only to get put back in the place where I belonged.

My new-found swagger as a jock had also changed the social landscape with my classmates. I hung out with new friends, teammates, cheerleaders and I became an item of attraction for the opposite sex. As we headed out of town for Oregon I feared that I would fall from grace with this heady crowd. And, I would have to leave my significant other behind as well.

For the first time in my life I wrote love letters, but rarely got one in return. We had 'in care of' postal addresses through our orchard owners and most often the mail would not catch up to our travels. The lyrics of my favorite music had new meaning and created mysterious new hormone infusions which were up to now non-existent. I dreaded the perceived separation from my new social standing and I knew that the next three months would move relentlessly slow. Even though the money was good and my bank account was the envy of my friends, the means of its accumulation was a subject that I didn't like to share or talk about much. There was always the back-handed innuendo of various uses and meanings of the word cherry.

I did however, survive that seemingly unending summer and excitedly endured the long trip home for the beginning of my last year of high school.

More recent times have allowed me to relish the participation of my daughters and later, grandchildren in sporting events, class plays, music, both instrumental and voice. Such a heavy emphasis is now placed on off season club sports, private lessons, and year around practice. I think it puts a huge burden on a young person's shoulders to stay in the game and pressure to always perform at high levels in order to make the team or stay competitive. I also became a basketball coach and soccer coach at the club level and could share horror stories about being vilified as a coach by parents who felt that I wasn't good enough to teach their daughters at the highest level of skills they thought imperative to their kid's success in life.

In one particular club sport soccer season, a new coach from Jamaica arrived in our area and claimed to be the end all for coaching soccer. He was allowed during the tryouts to hand pick his team, mostly with girls who were also on the high school team. If I chose to continue coaching a team, I was left with the leftovers to form my team. My youngest daughter was a terrific soccer player, and quit that team and joined mine, along with the young women who didn't make the cut. To get enough players to form my team, I had to scout nearby high schools, for kids who had not made the cut on their clubs.

As we neared the fall club season, the organizing soccer group set up the various conferences and game scheduling. Of course, we were placed in the same group as the team that I had been excluded from. They were on our schedule to play the second game of the season, the same weekend that I had to be absent because I had to take my middle daughter to her move into her first year of college at Chapman University in Anaheim, California.

We hooked a small trailer with her stuff and headed west. That was the early days of cell phones that were about the size of one's forearm. While driving between Las Vegas and California, in the middle of the desert, I was able to get a signal if I stopped and got out of the car. I called home because I was so curious about the game's outcome. My daughter answered the phone and my first question was, "how did it go?" Her reply was, "Dad, we kicked their ass." I quickly became Chevy Chase, in the "Bad News Bears," hopping around the desert sand like a crazy man, totally bonkers about a 3-0 win.

How incredibly out of control the emphasis on excelling in sports and other activities has become. I think of the parents who cheated to get their kids in prestigious colleges. How insane that some professional athletes make more annually than the annual budgets of many small towns, more than the average citizen would make in 10 lifetimes. I saw small glimpses of the craziness while coaching 50 years ago.

Chapter Twenty-Six

By the time we arrived home, two days before school began, football practice had been underway for two weeks. My lofty status hadn't carried over from my previous athletic heroics. Dale Mullen was all healed up from his shoulder injury and fresh off a sterling summer of baseball and was once again the darling of the coaching staff.

The saving grace for me was the school's hiring of a new head football coach, Ralph Pucci. It appeared that he was not all caught up in the Who's Who of DHS sports and social circles, and he seemed to be excited that I showed up, even though a few weeks tardy. I had grown a couple of inches and had put on fifteen or twenty pounds of muscle. Lifting several tons of fruit boxes every day of the summer had made me fairly lean and hardened and had provided me with significant back and leg strength.

Coach Pucci had implemented many new aspects of the Winged T and added a lot of triple option to the offense. I had absolutely zero knowledge of the correlation between physical gifts and their applications to position strengths, but I could flat out run and administer the triple option. I started every game at quarterback and had an awesome year both in the performance and self-esteem departments.

I had pretty much metamorphosed from who I had perceived myself to be to who and what I had become. However, I never seemed to recover as a student from my sixth grade abuse and was very average in the classroom. I was pretty convinced that I was not very smart and struggled with science and math curricula. I found it more comforting to associate with others who labored with their books and avoided those whom I perceived to be much smarter than I. As a jock in those mid-western cultures, schools were actually allowed to administer rules and discipline. I was about as straight as you could get, but not so hot academically. My football position coach and basketball coach knew that my teammates were hitting some of the rural roads and smoking a few cigarettes and drinking a few Schlitzs. The coach pulled me aside along with others on the team and declared that anyone caught doing either or anyone not passing classes were not welcome on the team. And, they meant it. Consequently, all of that bad behavior and poor studies disappeared in a flash. I even managed to keep my scholarly head above water.

I flourished with my participation in extracurricular activities involving myself in singing groups, forensics, school drama club, student council and just about anything to avoid the academic side of school. I did manage to graduate at the midpoint academically of my class and chose to go to a small, easy to qualify for college in northern Missouri with a small athletic scholarship.

My senior year was a watershed of social issues and self-esteem reflection. I was voted by my classmates as the most representative senior of DHS and was elected president of the senior class and the captain of the basketball team. We had about 100 in our senior class and I liked every one of them and treated each of them in a congenial, friendly manner.

Some of the prominent memories of one's high school years are easy to recall because of the magnitude of their effect on their life. Often it is a tragedy that takes a friend far too early or a best friend moving away that has an impact for years if not for all of one's life. One such event had a significant impact on the professional music scene in the late 50's and created legendary musical spin offs for a few years.

Rock and roll music was building a full head of steam by the late 50's to the chagrin of the parents of teenagers of that era. They cringed at the gyrations of Elvis Presley and the big hairdos of the musicians of that era. They expressed the fear that Satan certainly was an influence on rock culture. Television was still a relatively new phenomenon and young people had to sneak home early from school to watch American Bandstand hoping to not get left behind in learning the latest songs, names of artists, and the in-vogue dance style that changed monthly.

During the winter of 1959, a few of my friends scored tickets to a music concert at the Surf Ballroom in Clear Lake, Iowa, nearly 200 miles from Denison. I had three big things that blocked my path to joining the fray. My parents hated rock and roll. The concert was on a school night, Monday, and there was a blizzard developing. In spite of all of my attempts to cajole them into letting me go, I lost the battle and my five friends went without me.

Little did we know at the time, that was the day the music died. Buddy Holly, Richie Valens, and P.J. Richardson, the "Big Bopper" all performed along with a few others. Following the concert, those three, along with their pilot, chose to fly to their next venue instead of taking their tour bus because the heater was not working. Early in the morning of February 3, 1959, the plane crashed, killing all on board. I did manage to drive to the crash site along with some friends two days later to join hundreds of other young fans to look at the crash site.

One of the consolation prizes was that my best friend, Tom, brought a printed program from the event which he gave to me the next day before anyone knew what had happened. Years later, in 2013 I attended a Broadway production of The Buddy Holly Story at the Temple Buell Theater in Denver. A terrific impersonator of Holly portrayed his life on stage. Near the end of the show the cast re-staged an enactment of his last concert. The house lights dimmed and the ushers ascended the aisles passing out printed programs of that last night. When I saw it, I was sure that I had seen it before. The next day I searched through my high school memorabilia and found the original that was an exact match, different paper and the obvious wear of some 50 years, and the typeface and photo reproduction differences.

Over the years, I've occasionally played games of 'Can you top this,' or 'Truth or Dare,' and the participants can't quite believe the tragic story, or that I was there the day the music died even if a day or so late.

I knew very little about college, feared the challenge of succeeding academically at the next level and dreaded the thought of leaving my cocoon of comfort that my successes had provided. I had a very serious girlfriend who was going to an all women Catholic school for nursing and I knew that spending our last summer together before heading off to college was not going to happen for me. Like so many small-town jocks that planned to be the big man on campus once they arrived at their college, I would be in for one large maladjustment to my university football experience.

The end of May arrived, I said my sad goodbyes to my sweetheart and I, once again, became a fruit tramp. My oldest sister had gotten married that year, so the remaining five of us filled up the Chevy and headed west.

I remember very little about that summer except for the dread that fall of heading off to a college academic environment for which I was so ill prepared.

Following that summer and once back in Denison, my parents packed all that they could into a U-Haul truck and moved to Boulder, Colorado, and I headed to Northwest Missouri State College in Marysville, Mo. I had an athletic scholarship that covered the cost of my tuition and board, but I had to pay for my housing. My football experience was short-lived. The promise of a freshman team (common in college at that time) evaporated into a 'we are all one' scenario where I found myself on a team of whipping boys and doing tackling drills and getting my brains hammered.

One day I found myself in the queue for a tackling drill and I couldn't remember how I had gotten in line from the previous body assault. When I confronted a coach about the freshmen team and about doing position specific drills such as quarterback, he pretty much convinced me that I was a pussy and not worthy of my scholarship. That was the end of my athletic career, prompting a withdrawal from school and a move back to Denison, living alone in our vacant home and looking for a grunt job. The upside of that equation was that I was able to withdraw as a student in good standing, which eventually allowed me to transfer to the University of Colorado in the Spring semester of the following year. Without that blessing, I would never have been admitted due to my poor high school grades.

After leaving Northwest Missouri State, I went back to Denison even though my entire family was gone to Colorado. I went to our vacant home for a place to live and latched on to a job at the newspaper where my dad had worked. I got a job as the nighttime photographer—on call from 5:00 p.m. until eight in the morning. I usually had very little to do unless something newsworthy happened that needed photo enhancement during the after hours. When a call came during that time frame it usually wasn't for a good reason. It would lead me to a home with a domestic dispute, a fire somewhere on a property or some kind of an accident. One such call came to me after midnight alerting me of a car accident several miles east of Denison. When I arrived at the scene it became obvious that there had been a lot of carnage. Before the Interstate system came about in the early 60's almost all of Iowa's highways were two lane roads with rounded concrete shoulders that edged the right of way and limited wandering onto the shoulder of the road.

The accident had taken place on an elevated bridge with a left hand downward turn. When I got out of my car, the highway patrolman strongly suggested that I might not want to take photos of the scene, but with my Press Pass I was allowed to make my own decision. In hindsight, I wished I had opted out. A semi-tractor trailer had stalled on the bridge at the curved portion and hadn't had enough inertia to make it down to where the guard rails had ended. A convertible with 6 teens at an obviously high rate of speed heading in the same direction had gone underneath the trailer, shearing the convertible top and most of the heads of the occupants.

There were bodies and decapitated heads strewn about the road and massive amounts of blood on the road. All six perished. I became very nauseous and lost my dinner and was unable to complete my task, save for one photo from a distance lacking any clear image of the disaster that had taken place. PTSD had not yet been identified, but when I learned of it many years after the Viet Nam war, I knew that I suffered with it and occasionally still do.

Dick Knowles, the paper owner, was very perceptive of what I had encountered and told me that he had an opening for a reporter. I gladly took the job and wrote high school sports stories for the remainder of my last days in Denison. Little did I know at the time that this minor excursion into the news media would eventually lead to an interest and a B.S. degree in Journalism from the University of Colorado 6 years

later and enough diversions along the way to stop a
train.

Chapter Twenty-Seven

"You're in the army now,
you're not behind a plow.
You're diggin a ditch,
You'll never get rich.
You're in the army now."
Isham James
You're in the Army Now

In hindsight, I now realize how much damage had been done to my intellectual pursuits. My 'in good standing' status at NWMS allowed me to matriculate at the University of Colorado the following semester where I never would have been admitted out of high school. However, I began once again my college career absent any diversions with athletics.

I had very little confidence that I could survive the academics and certainly didn't enhance that perception by overly pursuing my studies. I joined a fraternity, became a partier on steroids and was soon given a pink slip with 43 credit hours and a .923 GPA. Within three weeks of my probation, I got a 'Greetings' notice from my Uncle Sam and soon was drafted in 1963 to the United States Army.

I went through basic and AIT at Ft. Leonard Wood, Missouri, and on to artillery training for deployment preparation to Viet Nam in Ft. Sill, Oklahoma. Little did I know that an incident during basic that got me in hot water with our CO, led to his suggesting an application for an 'early out' from my active duty obligation, solely for the purpose of returning to academia and completion of a degree. As compensation for not fulfilling my active duty, two-year commitment, I had to commit to six years of reserve duty with the Colorado National Guard and waive all rights to GI benefits. Anything short of college matriculation would have landed me back in the military and likely duty in Southeast Asia.

Chapter Twenty-Eight

"They say that in the Army
the coffee is mighty fine.
Well, it's good for cuts and bruises,
but it tastes like turpentine.
Oh, I don't want no more army life,
Gee Ma, I wanna go home."
Author unknown
Gee Ma, I wanna go home

I received my draft notice in February. There is an end-of-this-world feeling when that 'greetings and salutations' arrives in your mailbox. It is not something that you can ignore or pretend that you didn't get. The draft in those days was reinstated to help provide enough troops to stage a foreign war and 2.2 million young men would be drafted over a ten year span out of a pool of 27 million. So, I wasn't alone in the frightful state of mind that persisted in that era of American history.

There was enough angst about the ticket to Viet Nam that many, mostly false, schemes were concocted to either fail the physical exam, or make plans to falsely acquire an un-draftable status like being married or full time matriculation at a university. I cooked up such a scheme with my best friend, for me to marry his girlfriend. Most such plans hatched during inebriated, after party crazy talk. Many young men burned their draft cards and over 100,000 took up residence in Canada or Sweden.

After doing any number of things to assure that I would fail my physical, I traveled one afternoon to Denver for my first exposure to military style medical procedures. After passing the physical exam with surprise, chagrin, and disappointment I was asked to report for active duty in mid-June. The night before leaving, I went to Estes Park, a nearby resort town at the base of Longs Peak snuggled within the Rocky Mountains. Having been there a few times to drink 3.2 beer (legal then for 18 year olds) at some rocking places like Jack Snax, the Rock Inn, the Cowboy Bar and others, I was well aware of what I wanted to do—to get drunk enough, hoping somehow I could avoid the inevitable.

I managed the first part, but the inevitable was just that, unavoidable.

I managed somehow to make it to my parents' home, crash and be awakened by them at 5:30 a.m. for a trip to Union Station in Denver for a troop train embarking for Kansas City. Hangover doesn't properly describe my condition that morning as my parents drove me to Denver. Along with the katzenjammer, I had terrible anxiety and a foreboding about the goodbyes to come that morning. After 20 some years of being very close to them, that day was my first real goodbye.

The train was filled with only poor bastards just like me, most of whom were draftees and many that were RA's meaning that they had chosen to join for a four-year stint compared to a US (draftee) two year gig. There was a sameness among us that displayed mostly anxiousness, bewilderment, and fear of the Viet Nam unknown.

In 1963 the United States' commitment to solving the fear of Communism spreading from North to South Viet Nam called for massive amounts of military buildup in the United States. It was a very controversial endeavor by the US and promulgated numerous protests, campus rioting, burning flags, sit ins and numerous other forms of dissent that rivaled the tenacity of the protests following Trump's victory in 2016 and the summer riots of 2020 causing some two billion dollars of property damage and the loss of many lives, some 70-plus law enforcement personnel included. Shortly after the train left Denver, the diner cars opened their doors for breakfast. I wasn't feeling too well, but I do remember feeling hungry. I went through my first military buffet style feeding line and was served some of my first army style grub, heavy on runny eggs, hash browns and bread. Servers would put the food on a metal tray with little choice on our part as to the quantity served. I managed to eat just enough to get a gagging reflex, but managed to hold on to the groceries. I didn't eat much of what I had on the tray and proceeded to the busing station to unload the mostly uneaten portion. When I arrived at the station there was an NCO (non-commissioned officer) standing there. I had no idea what an NCO was or how I would loathe them until I became one.

He asked me what the hell I was doing with the food on the tray. When I told him that I wasn't hungry, a big mistake, he dragged me back to the table and forced me to follow the mantra of "take all you want, but eat all you take." I managed to force it down and get out of the diner before the eruption. The train arrived early the next morning and upon disembarking we were shuttled to a bus station where we were herded into Greyhound style buses for the last leg from KC to Ft. Leonard Wood, Missouri.

So far, I was one day into my stay with Uncle Sam, traveling on an air conditioned train and then an air conditioned bus thinking it wasn't all too bad. We arrived at the army base mid-afternoon and were quickly forced from the buses along with our meager luggage and commanded to line up in some formation alongside the buses, about 15 or so buses parked after disembarking the new troops. It was unbearably hot and humid and I thought the intense heat was caused by our proximity to the buses and their engine heat. Once away from the buses, I realized that it was summer in southern Missouri, nearly a hundred degrees and very humid. I felt like passing out or passing on, but didn't want to elicit the wrath of the uniforms barking out instructions.

The first two weeks were filled with supply lines for issuing our gear, fatigue boots, t-shirts, and olive drab clothing, a footlocker for storing our worldly possessions and shoeshine kit. Of course, our hairdos would radically change from the duck tails, Mohawks, and long sideburns to being replaced by the universal military style of 'high and tight,' or a basic head shave. We also did medical testing for who knows what and received inoculations for every possible disease known to western civilization. We were also issued an M-14 rifle, helmet liner and helmet which would suffice for 90 percent of our head gear for the following few months.

The inoculations were administered in bunches by going through a gauntlet of medics who shot the various concoctions into our arms with air guns. I don't know what all of them were, but I do know that we received shots for smallpox, polio, mumps, flu, malaria, chickenpox, and measles and eight or ten more for who knows what. A number of GI's got really sick after the jabbs and some guys had swollen red welts all over their bodies. A few were dubbed as the "sick, lame and lazy" and presumably sent home or to hospitals. Each day began with revelry and much shouting and formations, incessant standing at attention in the blazing sun, and barrack inspections. I thought it was all pretty silly, but didn't think it was that demanding but for the heat and humidity.

We were just into our third week and I was already counting the days until the end of boot camp. The next morning we were rousted out at sunrise in our full gear complement and put into a company formation of four platoons, Delta Five Two in our collective case: Delta company of the 5th Battalion, Second Regiment. We joined up with the three other companies in our battalion and began to learn to march in formation. We were led by flag bearers and a drum corps. At the upper tip of one of the flags was a cylindrical object with the number 'one' clearing visible. When I inquired as to the meaning of the number, thinking maybe we were already number one for some mystical reason, I was informed that the number represented the start of the first week of basic training—12 weeks, minus one day of misery to go. I hadn't realized that those first weeks were needed to process enough troops to build a regiment sized group to conduct basic training, from start to finish at the same time. During that wartime, there were several military bases that also conducted basic training. In a few short weeks, another regiment would begin its training at Ft. Leonard Wood. Occasionally, we would come into brief contact with the newbies and demonstrate massive amounts of gloating at their neophyte shortcomings, along with a 'you-ain't-seen-nothing-yet' arrogance.

Just a short time ago I had been a frivolous college frat boy shooting for the moon, occasionally shooting them and now a soldier with absolutely no control over my circumstances. I looked for a Thesaurus-appropriate word for misery but could not find one that could properly express my state of mind. I made fun of endless routines that are used to instill discipline and fortitude, like an entire battalion being commanded to 'take your seats' at some educational assembly, and repeating the standing and sitting until the leader could only hear 'one ass' in unison as we took our seats. Endless 'fall out' for barrack inspections at all hours of the day or night. Marching in formation to a cadence, carrying a rifle at right shoulder arms, covering two or three miles and then being commanded to halt without one single forward leaning motion from any soldier, and then repeating the process until we had not one leaner.

Somewhere in the mid part of Basic, I found myself getting really pissed at guys who just didn't get it or were incapable of performing at that level. There was a term, 'BOLO,' an innocuous word that resulted in the ominous procedure of being taken from the company and sent to the newest regiment to start over. The threat was always there and pretty much kept everyone in line except for those who just couldn't adjust, shoot, sweat, read or oblige. I was one of those who just couldn't shoot. After some serious sweating, the rifle qualification exercise, hitting at least fifty percent of the targets anywhere from 50 to 500 meters distant, I realized that I couldn't see the targets at that distance and didn't spot the man-sized silhouette targets until the sun flashed from their surface when they dropped back down. I was sent to the infirmary for an eye exam, new glasses, and a clear world for the first time in many years. No BOLO for me. I passed with a score of 78 out of 100 and was given a marksmanship medallion.

At the midpoint of basic I started putting the pieces together and subtly striving to be the best that I could be. I think the toughness I learned in my fruit picking days, loading tons of cherries, and sweating in the summer sun along with quarterbacking a football team and captaining a basketball team still resided in my brain. We were told that one troop from each company would be designated as the Outstanding Trainee of our cycle. There were five events called the PCPT or physical combat proficiency test, consisting of a 72 rung horizontal ladder, a dodge run and jump, a forty yard low crawl, a grenade throw, followed by a one mile run in combat gear. They were rated by the speed of each event and the accuracy of the grenade throw, a total of 500 points, the maximum attainable score.

We practiced dry runs many times and I aspired to win the award for our battalion. On the day of the finals, I was brimming with confidence having watched my peers and assessing the likelihood of any serious competition. The battalion was about 200 strong and I only saw those 50 or so in Delta company do their thing but I didn't know much about those from Alpha, Bravo or Charlie. I had completed three of the events with a perfect score and when doing the low crawl and about to finish when someone stood on my shoulder for about 10 seconds impeding my progress. I finished the mile run with a perfect time and ended up with 495 out of 500 points. My platoon DI was Sergeant Walter Demetro who thought I was the cat's meow because of my competitive attitude. One day when shouting out my service number to him, a thrice daily requirement before entering the chow hall, he expressed major chagrin when he realized that I was a US (draftee) and not a RA. It was he who had stood on my shoulder during the low crawl which led to Tommy Hughes winning the award with 497 points. We had tied in all of the other events, but I had vanquished him in the mile run by 10 seconds.

Chapter Twenty-Nine

"The war is over, turn around
Lay your weapons on the ground
The smoke is fading, before the light
The dead are becoming back to life"
The War is Over
Bethel Music

I could easily pen a few thousand words about my military days but that would be another book in itself. Suffice it to say that I completed basic, AIT (Advance Individual Training) with a MOS (Military Occupational Speciality) as a clerk typist, quickly changed to combat artillery where I became a staff sergeant and section chief of an eight inch Self Propelled Howitzer unit. I dodged the Viet Nam bullet twice by being granted the early release to return to college, cutting short active duty, but requiring me to complete my military obligation in a reserve unit for five more years in a howitzer company. Our unit was put on STRAC status, doubling our time commitment for training and a likely ticket to Viet Nam. Shortly after receiving our new STRAC status, President Lyndon Johnson chose to not run again for the presidency and called an end to the war. I have been stood up a few times in life, but this 'standing down' was a great relief.

Ironically, some of my reserve duty call ups mirrored what is going on today in our fruited plains—riots, looting, burning government buildings and police stations. For several weeks, garbed in riot gear with a rifle and fixed bayonet (no ammo allowed because of a National Guard event in Kent State University in Ohio that left a few rioting students dead from a guardsman's rifle). We spent our days in pinzer formations unblocking roadways and trying to prevent campus and nearby businesses from being burned to the ground and structures looted and ransacked. You would think that we might have learned our lesson and made chaos like this a distant memory in our history books. Reflecting on my short military career it is abundantly clear, at least to me, that it would be almost impossible to not acknowledge the profound, positive impact it has on one's character and firmly establishes a crystal clear appreciation for the concept of patriotism for the United States of America. All who serve sacrifice in some way; an enormous life detour, time away from loved ones and family, disruption of life timelines, bad habits formed, very low pay. But, love for country and our flag becomes a badge of honor that most who served would be willing to answer the call again to defend those things, such as our freedoms that we hold so dearly.

As I reflect on my life, there are a few outstanding individuals who had a subtle but profound influence on me along with a few events that were necessary and severe course corrections; detours without which I may have run off of the cliff.

One such detour were those years without summers where I learned the valuable lesson of survival, hard work and the commensurate reward of perseverance—the long days without cell phones, iPads, TV, with only the transistor radio, battery life notwithstanding, for mental diversion. I think those days forced us to be 'close' as a family and we had to rely on each other for companionship. In reflecting on the dearth of electronic diversions from those days, it reminded me of an event in the life of Cory Ten Boom, in her book, *"The Hiding Place,"* where she describes the early days of Holland's occupation by the Nazis.

As people volunteered to move away or were forced away because of their ethnicity, they would receive gifts from the departing friends. One such gift was an old tube type radio. They had to hide it away during the day and the entire family and refugees living with them would bring it out in the evening and rejoice being with the entourage just listening to that radio.

Put that in the perspective of today's family and the likelihood of a family doing any such thing today without a rebellion. I remember a recently conducted survey that polled the scenarios of today's nuclear family. One question was, "How many days a week do you set down with your family for a meal or activity?" A not-to-small percentage replied that it <u>never</u> happened but for an occasional holiday event.

Chapter Thirty

"You raise me up so I can stand on mountains,
you raise me up to walk on stormy seas,
I am strong when I am on your shoulders,
you raise me up to more than I can be."
Josh Groban
You Raise Me Up

I mentioned in an early chapter the sculpting that takes place in any given person's life that mold them into the sculptures and beings that serve them for life. Often, flawed pieces of art, but intact and functional. I have assessed some of those events and persons that were the craftsmen in my molding. I think the metaphor of art creation is a great one to describe human beings. None are the same, none are perfect. Some are works of art, some are seriously flawed and not pleasant. Some are colorful, others dull. Many are hard to understand and cause us to question the creator. All are original and many have numbered copies—not as valued as the initial product.

As human beings we have the priceless opportunity to take the original and reshape it with our own hands or to have restorative functions performed by those special events and people when the colors and tapestry fade and unravel. Too many are created in environments by people who failed art class and are cast aside with little hope of being found and restored, or handed off to a disinterested third, or more, party who disregard any attempt at mending. Oftentimes the fixes are attempted with toxic paints making the object worse than the original. Too many are discarded to the landfills of humanity.

When I reflect on the events and persons that sculpted me it is clear that the consequence parts of the equation were rarely a moment in time, but most often a long process such as healing from surgery, making it through college, military, our wedding, the addition of children to our family. Eventually, grandchildren. The remarkable people contacts were often brief and one-time encounters when something they said or shared had a profound effect at just the right time.

I failed both English composition and first semester Spanish in college. I had to repeat both subjects to satisfy those mandatory credits. I thought both teachers were awful which could have been part of the reason for my failed grade. When I repeated those classes the following semester, my new English teacher told me that I was a terrific writer and my new Spanish teacher told me I was doing so well that I should consider Spanish as a major or minor. What changed? I believe the answer was that my first classes were taught by people who shouldn't have been there and the following semester classes were led by professionals who loved what they did and wanted to have a positive influence on their students. Being exposed to both types of professors was a lesson that I didn't fully appreciate at the time but discovered its significance years later.

One of my favorite collegiate mentors, Dal Ward, was the head football coach of the University of Colorado Buffaloes for 11 years. Back in those days coaches weren't pampered and privileged as they are today. They also had to teach classes and Dal happened to be a teacher in the Physical Education department where I took my mandatory PE class. The end of the semester following my initial crash and burn startup semester found me with a 1.8 GPA at semester's end with a B in the PE class. I needed to have a 2.0 GPA to become active in my fraternity, and needed an A in the PE class. So I went on a plea bargain mission to coach Ward.

He was amazingly affable when I told him of my request for him to change my PE grade from a B to an A, which would just get me by. After my request he asked me where I was from and when I told him Denison, Iowa, he asked me if I knew the Denison football coach, Ralph Pucci. When I told him I quarterbacked the Monarchs we got to be real cozy. He called my old coach and they chatted, presumably about my character and attitude. When he finished with the call he took me on a tour of the trophy center and pointed out a number of great successes that his teams had at CU. When we were finished, he honored my request and I got my 2.0. High stakes at the time in my collegiate pursuits.

I learned more about Dal as the years went on and I became a bleeding Silver and Gold Buffalo fan. Dal was one of the first coaches to recruit African American athletes in the days when few schools would even consider such a thing. On one particular trip to Salt Lake City for a game against Utah, he was informed that the black athletes would not be allowed to make the trip. He personally stood his ground and suggested the game be called off. The Utes rescinded the demand and the Buffs headed West. Once in Salt Lake the team checked in to their hotel and were informed that blacks would not be allowed to stay at the hotel. Dal responded, "If they can't stay here, then neither can we and we'll just get on a bus, catch a plane and head back to Boulder." The staff relented. There were two African Americans on the team, Frank Clarke and John Wooten, and the hotel offered them to stay together in the 'crow's nest' of the hotel. Again, Dal responded, "Johnny is an offensive lineman and he'll room with Bob Solerno, as he always does. Frank is a wide receiver and he'll room with Dusty Rhodes." That was that.

I felt privileged to have known this great man and to have my life impacted by his act of kindness to me. The outcome of becoming an active member, and no longer a pledge, in my Delta Upsilon fraternity, through no fault of Dal Ward, would clearly accelerate my path to scholarly destruction.

There were a few other mentors and human light beams throughout my life and a few new ones come along every now and then.

A few of those profound role models were very spiritual people. In spite of my 10 years of perfect attendance at Sunday School, I knew many Bible stories and could recite scripture, but during my early college years, I drifted away from my faith primarily because I thought it would interfere with my collegiate craziness. I hung out with people who had either abandoned their theological virtue or had never had it in the first place. Churchy friends were not fun and were preachy. Somewhere in between failing my early college years, Army, and then my academic resurrection I realized I had done enough self-inflicted damage that I began a subtle search for some authentic meaning to life.

During those foggy days I was blessed to have met a few people that were perceptive enough to know that I was lost and searching for some real purpose to my life. I thank God for his divine orchestration of those chance encounters that got me back on the rails. I found a church near campus that attracted quite a number of coeds which likely appealed to me as much as did the theology. I eventually joined and became a member that is still going after almost 60 years. My life-long marriage began there and my three daughters were involved in the youth program, baptized, and married either there or by pastors from the church at a different location.

We have been blessed by our association with the church on several occasions when near tragedies threatened our well-being—car accidents, breast cancer, parental death, nearby wildfires, a major flood, and a close to death event with our youngest daughter when she was two, along with the general malaise of survival that comes with life.

Like most young people we search and follow so many different paths in life. Yogi Berra once said, "when you come to a fork in the road, take it." There have been many forks in the road and my discernment wasn't always the correct choice. But somehow, if we are fortunate we end up where we are supposed to end up. I know people who take personal credit for their arrival at the mountain top. I choose to take no credit for that, but assign that serendipity to the above-mentioned people and to the Spirit of God who is the only way to the mountain top.

Reflecting on my life has made it abundantly clear that no matter where you come from, what you look like, or what obstacles are placed before you, because of our God-given freedoms, anyone can succeed, but it won't be handed to you. The caveat is that we need the government to stay out of our way and not convince us that we need their subsidies and then become reliant on them instead of our own self-sufficiency. I can state for a fact that not one member of my birth family or my own children's families have ever received any form of government largess.

After being in college for a couple of years, I had found new friends mostly through my fraternity association. It is clear that as we advance through life, we continue to associate with the types of people with whom we are most comfortable. Up to that point in life, my BFF had been my neighborhood highschool friend, sports teammate, occasional church attender and just all around good guy, Tom Walker. Tom lived catty corner from me in a new home. He and his brother Dick were both adopted at birth and his parents both had issues with alcohol addiction. His mother would become overly controlling after drinking too much and would get verbally abusive with her sons.

My mom was pretty savvy about what was going on and with her heart of gold offered numerous times for Tom to eat with us and often to spend the night when things were bad at his home. We became like brothers and remained that way throughout high school and for years after. Tom joined the Marines right out of high school and we parted ways for eight or so years until one day when I received a call from him asking me to send bail. I did so without question and sent him enough money to get out of jail and a bus ticket to Colorado.

I had just purchased my first home, a rental income property that had four apartments and a main house with three bedrooms. I was still single at the time, so the intrusion worked out ok for a while.

He seemed to be into sobriety until one afternoon at FAC (known as Friday Afternoon Club). He went off the wagon, drank everything in my meager liquor cabinet and became very drunk and belligerent and had done some damage before I arrived home from work. I eventually had to get him enrolled in a mandatory rehab program that he hated me for. He eventually died from alcohol abuse some 10 years after that sad event and I sadly didn't find out until long after his death.

My other BFFs, two in all, were both fraternity related. One, like me who had significant financial struggles through their early lives. The University of Colorado is not one of those places that was easy to afford even in the 60's. Because of its geographic beauty, abundant skiing, and party life, it attracted and still has a certain party scene student body from all over the country and world. Most of my acquaintances came from out of state, arrived each fall with new cars and pre-paid their tuition, books, and fraternity social expenses. I, on the other hand, worked as full time as possible, as a food service employee of CU, a sorority 'hasher,' (serving food, cleaning up, kitchen work).

No surprise that my best buddy in those early years was knitted from the same yarn. We were pledges together in the fraternity, hashed together, and dated in the same sorority.

Bob Hawkins, The Hawk was my attached-at-the-hip soulmate. We could never fully pay our fraternity debt until the following summer when we would pay it off with income from full-time summer employment, to the chagrin of the fraternity business manager. He just couldn't understand why our daddies just simply write a check.

We also both struggled with a huge imbalance of social vs. academic life, the social side almost always winning out. We always tried to run with the big dogs, and act like we were just like them. He had an old beater Chevy that we would nudge into service on weekends to the many ski areas in the nearby Rockies. We would wait near the ski patrol shacks in the morning, hoping to find a toboggan delivered, injured skier and barter for their no longer needed lift ticket.

We spent many nights in his car so we could ski the next day. On occasion, we would venture into ski lodges, find a hidden nook and crash on the floor for the night and see our friends the next day acting like we were cool and could go big on the skiing stage.

The Hawk and I were always scheming on ways to bust out of our poverty and make big, quick bucks. Most plans were pipe dreams at best, but we did have a few that worked for us. We got a wild idea to buy old Jeeps in the part of the country where they weren't as valuable as they are in ski country. We would go to the library and scan through newspaper classifieds in Nebraska and Iowa. When we found at least two Jeeps for sale we would buy a Greyhound bus ticket to the location near one of the Jeeps. We traveled together to the nearest town to the location of the Jeep, checked it out, bought it with some hard price negotiation and hopped in to go look at the others wherever they resided. Our goal was to buy four on each trip, tow one with the other back home and end up with four for sale. We did this very thing three or four times in a couple of years and made pretty good money, usually doubling, if not more than the buy/sell amount.

On one such trip over winter break, we bought four Jeeps and brought them back to Colorado. Of the four that we purchased, only one had a top, a CJ5 with a metal cab. The other three had no tops, so I ended up drawing the short straw and drove home in an open Jeep with another in tow. Wouldn't you know, we traveled over 500 hundred miles in a blizzard to get back home. We were forced to stop at a thrift store in Lincoln, Nebraska, where we bought several old blankets. I wrapped all of them around me as best as I could and still was able to steer and headed West. It's been far too many years ago to remember it clearly, but you can only imagine my description of that trip. 'Foxhole' situations can only make for some inseparable bonds between hole mates.

Hawk was a good artist and we spent several evenings designing an invention for automobiles that would have four triangular pieces with reflective glass on one side that stacked together and could be stored flat inside of a trunk. If car problems caused a stoppage on a highway, the driver could open the trunk, attach one of the units with a magnet to the rear of the car, and place the other three at intervals behind the car on their little jack stands to alert other cars. Beyond that we had no clue or connections on how to get the thing made or marketed. Hawk found a company that claimed to help with the development and marketing of pipe dream projects such as ours and we met with the rep, who turned out to be the chief crook and bottle washer of the whole shebang.

We nearly flipped when he offered to build and market our idea for a mere $1200. We were both working full time by then, but that was more than a massive amount for us to assemble. The 'rep,' Mr. Haskell Shott, painted a rosy picture that was too good to pass up, so we emptied bank accounts, piggy banks, and any place we could find a spare dime and went for broke. Not much happened and within a few months of trying to re-trace Mr. Shott, we discovered that he had moved his 'company' to the Midwest and left us broke and heartbroken. We tried to contact him, but you know the answer to that endeavor.

My dad, who worked for Dow Chemical at Rocky Flats, Colorado, would often be rewarded along with many other Dow employees with gift premiums for a certain number of accumulated hours of work without a lost time accident. He showed up from work one day with one such item—an accident prevention tool for cars, identical to the one that we had designed, manufactured by a company in the Midwest where good old Haskell had moved a few years before. To avoid throwing good money after bad, we chose not to retain a lawyer to the tune of a $2,500 fee to go after the crook. "Let the buyer beware."

I had way too many 'far out' experiences with Bob Hawkins over many years that could fill its own book.

Suffice it to say that we were cut from the same dime store cloth and somehow found a way to make a success out of life with less than favorable building blocks. Hawk was the best man at my wedding and was able to join us in a 25 year re dedication of our wedding vows with Suzi, along with our entire original wedding party. We stayed connected for almost all of 60 years. I got a phone call a short while ago from one of his progeny. He had died after a battle with a number of old man's afflictions. A part of me is gone. I often read the local obituaries, and realize that the lion's share are in my age group or older, but when a Bob Hawkins is the name attached to the obit, the reality of that loss is so much more profound.

I included this story in my book because it so well fits the theme of Never Summer. Looking back, I realized that I not only lost all of my summers for 13 years in the fruit orchards but also for all of my college years because I was always playing catch up to the curriculum and working all summer to stay out of debt. No, I don't think your college loans should be forgiven!

One of my menial jobs during my college years was as a paperboy on wheels. I was hired by the Denver Post to deliver newspapers every day, without fail. I was experienced when I took the job, because I had a paper route as a kid, delivering daily from bags slung across the rear of my Schwinn bicycle, with my dad helping me Sunday mornings due to very large, heavy editions. This system was different. I drove about 60 miles per day mostly throwing each paper on the driveway of mostly rural subscribers. I delivered every afternoon around 4:00 p.m. and started at 2:00 a.m. on

Sunday mornings, finishing around 8:00. A big challenge every Sunday was after Saturday night fraternity parties.

I believe that God often ventures way off a given path to accomplish something of importance to one of His people of which we may never connect the dots within our lifetime. That path happened to be my motor route. I knew every one of my customers on a first-name basis, because I would have to stop once each month to collect money for their delivered subscription. Several of my customers were homesteaders in Boulder County, Colorado, who built their homes after acquiring the land many years earlier or inheriting it from ancestors. One such man, Tom Kirkmeyer, owned several hundred acres north of Boulder and lived near the end of my daily journey. Several times when I collected from him, I would plead with him to sell me a small chunk of his land so I could one day live in the country. He actually called me one day and told me there was a for sale sign on a small chunk of land just south of his place. At the time, I was working at my first post college job and about to give up being a paperboy. Suzi and I were recently married, living in my first house, and not liking the thought of raising a family in town near the university.

We took a Sunday drive and visited the piece of land. It had a dirt driveway, a dug well, and a septic on five acres with one almost dead tree, mostly sage brush, and a couple of acres of cattails. Butt ugly sort of fits. I was concerned about the heavy clay soil and worried that it might contain expanding components that made foundation construction problematic. I knew a geology student friend at the time who offered to come out and do soil sampling. He concluded that we would likely be safe to build and offered an aside comment about cattails, stating that when you have them and maybe want to build a pond, all that was required was to remove them to the depth of our choosing and voila, we would have a pond that would never be drained of water. Somehow we drew up enough courage and enough money to buy the land. In a few short years we had our first child and the longing to have a country home was getting stronger. I had a pretty good job by then and we found a futuristic architect that was one of the early proponents of solar, ecologically designed homes. He would design and build our home that we finished in 1975. Our three daughters grew up there, all went away to college, got married and eventually all ended up back in Colorado.

Paul Harvey's "Rest of the Story" aptly fits the description of our home that we now call the 'pound' or the 'commune.' Two of our three daughters now live on our property and we have turned it into a small farm, with Christmas trees, goats, chickens, turkeys, and a bunny farm. Five of our seven grandchildren are the farmers and help take care of the place. But for the paper route, who knows where home might have been.

Chapter Thirty-One

"I 'm going back to my country, cause I can't pay
my rent. I may not be completely broke,
brother I'm badly bent."
Badly Bent
Tractors

I recently flew to Washington state with my wife to purchase a car and then spent a week on a scenic run through the old fruit picking haunts of my youth. I visited orchards where we had labored, found a few of the old shacks that were our temporary shelters, and went to the school in Manson, Washington, where I had such a terrible time learning to be a student against difficult odds. It gave me an appreciation for the thousands of lowly paid migrants

who labor in our country to help put food on your table and on theirs.

I purchased that car online from a dealership in Anacortes, Washington. It was August of COVID year, 2020. My wife and I flew to Seattle and got a shuttle to Anacortes where we picked up the car. We spent several days in the area and I luxuriated in being a tourist. We took a whale-watching cruise and went directly by Burroughs Island when as a cherry picking kid my dad took us on a side trip between our work in Oregon and Wenatchee. My dad had a former student who was serving in the Coast Guard and was stationed on the island as the light house manager. He picked us up on a Coast Guard Cutter in Anacortes and ferried us to the lighthouse where we spent the night. My most vivid memory of that sidebar was walking on the beach below the lighthouse among the seals and kelp. I had purchased a cowboy cap pistol with belt and holster and a cowboy hat following The Dalles harvest. I remember wanting to wade in the water, so I removed my hat and holster and hung them on a pier post while wading. As young boys are want to do, I forgot about them until the next morning only to discover that high tide had taken away my cherished purchase.

After leaving Anacortes, I followed as much of our well-worn path as logistically feasible from 65 years hence and took my wife on a nostalgia trip to many of our old fruit tramp haunts.

I was stunned by how much had changed, but also by how much had not changed at all. I had an overwhelming anxiety of what people do today that my family did in the 40's and 50's. I spoke with an orchard owner on Wenatchee Heights and told him about my childhood sojourns. In those days, getting 5 cents a pound to harvest was the baseline, give or take half cent up or down. Out of curiosity, I asked the owner what they paid harvesters currently. His reply was 5 cents a pound. I love to eat dark cherries to this day, and I am always a bit stunned to pay between three and four dollars a pound at the supermarket knowing

that some poor migrant had labored for 5 cents a pound to get my cherries to the local Safeway. We ended up visiting several harvest venues on our way home to Colorado. It was an emotional and instructive venture in several ways. It was almost impossible to believe that we had ever endured so many summers of picking fruit. It almost seemed that I had read a novel about other people living our summer life in fruit orchards and it couldn't possibly have been my family that had done so. I almost felt sorry imagining reading about people who did what we did, lived where we did and traveled 1,750 miles in an old car, sans AC to get there. It gave me a completely different perspective of my dad whom I observed many times having 'ulcer attacks.' Or, him fretting over a stalled car in Winnemucca, Nevada, or Quartzite, Arizona, two of several places where we spent more than a full day waiting to get our car fixed. Try that today with four kids, no video games or cell phones.

Like many things in life when you are put to a challenge, going through the event is tedious, boring, and discouraging, but when one looks back, it is clear what great preparation it was for facing future obstacles that are inevitable. I, and none of my siblings ever loafed through life going from job to job. All of us were productive and resourceful and had good careers. We were never afraid to work or fearful of working hard. However, none of us ever performed slug work again like we had done in the orchards. Perhaps we had gotten our fill of stoop labor.

While visiting some of the old haunts, one was in full harvest mode with many pickers. I didn't feel smug about it, but certainly didn't envy their labors in the summer sun and wondered how they could endure such hard work 12 hours a day. Surreal.

Since that car harvesting trip almost two years ago, I have been in a very contemplative stage of my life cogitating over really deep, philosophical stuff. Some of this deep thought has been nudged by conversations with others who have explored their own lineage through some of the online genealogy platforms. I have spent many hours reflecting on my own life and how the many phases of life that one passes through over the course of one's timeline. In my case 80 years. I have heard sermons in church and have read various Bible passages that astonishingly seem as though they were destined for me to read or hear. Recently, a wildfire near our home totally destroyed over 1,000 private homes. We had to evacuate once again, just like one year ago with an earlier fire, both just one mile from our home. A flood in 2013 completely filled our basement and ruined a collection of memorabilia from our past and our home's mechanical systems. The Biblical stuff that has curiously crossed my pathway helps me deal with events in my life that were stunningly fearful and cause for reflection on many of God's Psalmic promises.

I am not by any means feeling unduly punished or fearful or part of that group portrayed in the book, ***Why Bad Things Happen to Good People.*** My favorite, all time book written by Philip Yancey, ***The Question That Never Goes Away,*** has more quotable life inspiring messages than any book I've ever read. Two, in particular, may or may not resonate with you, but here there are. "The God of 14 billion years since the beginning of the universe; the God of human history and its long prehistory; the God of the 7 billion rejoicing, suffering, hoping, aching people on our planet, none the less meets us personally, listens to what we say, is interested in who we are and is passionate about what we might become, and walks alongside us in the chances and challenges of life. It's outrageous, improbable, and true." And, "I believe that God will give us in each state of emergency as much power of resistance as we need. But, He will not give it in advance, so that we do not rely on ourselves, but on Him alone."

I have had a decent share of those experiences in my adult life and wish to share one of the most poignant events. Twenty two years ago, I received a lottery selection for a white water raft trip on the Yampa and Green Rivers. A 7 day, incredible gift of luck. Suzi had chosen not to go on that particular trip due to a scheduled annual mammogram appointment a day before we would return home. She insisted that I go, otherwise the entire trip for 18 people would be canceled because the trip leader had to prove their identity prior to launch.

The trip finishes at Dinosaur National Monument in western Colorado. As soon as we arrived there, prior to the invention of the cell phone, I found a pay phone, called home, and talked with my oldest daughter. She said that I needed to be home A.S.A.P., some 8 hour drive at night, because Suzi had received a positive diagnosis of a lump and would be at the clinic the next morning for a confirmation through biopsy for breast cancer. Sixteen agonizing, anxiety-filled hours later, we got a cancer positive report with a follow up medical visit to ascertain the extent of the cancer. That test showed both breast cancer and lymph node incursions. She was scheduled for an expedient surgical process to remove breast cancerous tissue and as many lymph node extractions as necessary.

She went through an intense year of radiation and chemotherapy, nutritional and every other intervention that we could possibly pursue. A year later she developed severe back pain in several areas around her spinal column and rib cage. Her oncologist was quite fearful that the cancer had metastasized in her spine and conducted some dye-infused x-rays to properly diagnose what had happened. I went in with her for the procedure and we had to wait a few hours for the report. I clearly remember getting some takeout food and going across the street from the clinic to a small park, to eat lunch and wait. I was so upset that I couldn't eat. I tried to put on a brave front, but failed miserably. We could hardly talk to each other without weeping.

We returned and awaited the visit and report from the oncologist. When he entered the room I tried to read his face and demeanor to assess the news before he could verbalize the results. He asked us if we wanted the good or bad news first. I don't remember which we chose, but he proffered the good news first. He informed us that the cancer had not spread to her spine (the good part) and the pain was being caused by numerous small fractures to the spine as a result of the intense exposure to radiation and chemo that had triggered osteoporosis. Only fully blessed and crazy people would jump for joy when they found out they had spinal fractures. Life changed in a big way in that moment along with the reality that Suzi was not out of the woods and would face a long recovery with a higher than likely possibility that the cancer could revisit us. Another Yancey quote says, "In the fury of crisis, three questions are essential 1) Who do I love, 2) What have I done with my life, 3) Am I ready for what is next." We both got recharged that day and we tried to grasp the essence of our lives. There have been studies conducted to understand the issue of pain both from a perspective of going it alone and then dealing with the same pain with another person holding your hand. Without exception, when one suffers alongside of you, the pain level is cut by half.

We were surrounded by caring, loving friends who expressed concerns and prayers on a daily basis. Two years into Suzi's journey with cancer we passed a milestone when her doctor suggested that she was doing well and had a fairly positive long term prognosis. I had been so overwhelmed with the support of her team that I wanted to thank them in a grand, collective manner. I organized an event for about 60 family and friends as a surprise event for Suzi to give us both a chance to laugh and cry and thank these wonderful people. It was just before Christmas. One of my daughters, Kelly lived nearby, Kate was in college in New Hampshire, and Kristy was a missionary in Hungary. My plan was to have all three daughters there, one, Kristy as a surprise to all who would attend.

I had all of the tables set with specific numbers of settings for the attendees. A good friend had taken Suzi out for an afternoon of fun and shopping and then delivered her to the already assembled group. Kristy, in spite of a 20 hour travel ordeal from Budapest and a terrible respiratory infection, managed to make it about 20 minutes before Suzi arrived. She was hidden away until Suzi arrived. She was overwhelmed with surprise and electric emotion at seeing all of our group gathered. I took her to our table, and I asked her if there was anything unusual about the table setting, something I'm not known for doing exactly right. She said it looked ok and hadn't noticed the one extra setting. When I probed her about it, she seemed puzzled, so I seated her while she covered her eyes and brought Kristy in. Words can't properly paint the picture of her expression of shock, joy, confusion, and tears. Fortunately, I had a good friend video tape the evening and he did a masterful job of capturing that moment. We have watched it a few times since and our reaction is always the same.

I am known for a penchant to speak at funerals, weddings, and other event gatherings, but I had a difficult time that night sharing my thoughts and words. When I spoke I mentioned that the collective gathering had likely uttered a thousand prayers for Suzi and our family, and I suggested that we may not have survived with one less prayer.

Chapter Thirty-Two

"In the beauty of the lilies, Christ was born across the sea.
With a glory in his bosom that transfigured you and me
As He died to make us holy, let us die that all be free.
While God is marching on."
Julia Ward Howe
Battle Hymn of the Republic

As my fingers tapped on my keyboard over a number of months, like most authors, I had second thoughts about my motivation and inspiration to go beyond the drudgery of fruit picking and seek wisdom through hard thought and divine intervention to enhance the book's message. While sifting through the challenges that an 80 year old faces with life in general and aging in general, I was constantly reminded of the many empirical state of affairs of our great nation.

The college days of the 60's launched my emotional and social involvement in civics, a curriculum once taught in our schools. I have been a keen observer over many years of the petri dish that is the United States of America. There are 195 sovereign nations in the world, many spawned in a similar manner as the US. If one wanted to pursue a massive history project by studying the history of each nation, they would learn of the vagaries of each country--the motivation for their actuation, the masterminds of the effort, the pitfalls, and detours in their construction, and perhaps a few revolutions to help shape their destinies.

At their onset, most nations believe in some form of justice that links rational and natural law, fairness and divine order. Their ideals are set in motion and the blind lady holding the scale and sword watches it all unfold.

I don't know about many other countries, but I am intensely aware of her scale balancing act in the United States. It is clear that her scales are rarely in balance, but both trays change their vertical position and balance over extended periods of time, in the case of our country, with massive events like world wars, the Civil War, 9/11's and elections.

Another metaphor that may be a bit more graphically clear is that of a pendulum. An instrument that makes very huge swings from left to right. Swings that represent the enormous ebb and flow of a country's culture.

In my book I refer to some of the scale's imbalance changing over my lifetime and the subsequent upshot of those social impacts. A recent email from a friend included an audio file of a radio broadcast by Paul Harvey, likely one of the greatest newscasters of all time. It was broadcast in 1965, entitled, "If I Were the Devil."

If I were the devil,
If I were the prince of darkness,
I'd want to engulf the whole world
in darkness

And I would have a third of its real estate

173

and four-fifths of its population,

But I wouldn't be happy until I had seized
the ripest apple on the tree, thee.
So, I'd set about however necessary
to take over the United States.

I'd subvert the churches first.
With the wisdom of a serpent,
I would whisper to you as I whispered
to Eve, "Do as you please."
To the young, I would whisper that
The Bible is a myth.
I would convince them that man created
God instead of the other way around.
I would confide that what is bad is good,
and what is good is "square."

And the old I would teach to pray after me,
"Our father who art in Washington."
And then, I'd get organized.
I'd educate authors in how to make lurid
literature exciting so that anything else
would appear dull and uninteresting.
I'd threaten TV with dirtier movies
and vice versa.

I'd peddle narcotics to whom I could.
I'd sell alcohol to ladies and gentlemen
of distinction.
I'd tranquilize the rest with pills.

If I were the devil, I'd soon have

families at war with themselves,
churches at war with themselves,
and nations at war with themselves
until each in its turn was consumed.

And with promises of higher ratings,
I'd have mesmerizing media fanning the flames.

If I were the devil, I would encourage schools
to refine young intellects but neglect
to discipline emotions. Just let those run
wild until before you knew it, you'd
have to have drug sniffing dogs and metal
detectors at every schoolhouse door.

Within a decade, I'd have prisons overflowing.

I'd have judges promoting pornography.

Soon, I could evict God from the courthouse,
and then from the schoolhouse and then
from the houses of Congress.

And, in His own churches I would substitute
psychology for religion and deify science.
I would lure priests and pastors into
misusing boys and girls and church money.

If I were the devil, I'd make the symbol of Easter
an egg, and the symbol of Christmas a bottle.

If I were the devil, I would take from those who
have

**and I would give to those who wanted.
Until I killed the incentive of the ambitious.**

**And what will you bet I couldn't get whole
states to promote gambling as the way to get rich.**

**I would caution against extremes in hard work,
in patriotism, in moral conduct.**

**I would convince the young that your marriage
is old fashioned, that swinging is more fun, that
what you see on TV is the way to be.**

**And thus I could undress you in public, and
I could lure you into bed with diseases for which
there is no cure.**

**If I were the devil,
I'd keep right on doing what he's doing.**

I think Harvey's broadcast that day clearly suggests that the scales of Themis and the moral compass of a nation is commensurate with the enormous swings between good and evil, and proportionate to the health of the Church. Harvey suggests that for evil to proliferate, attacks on the Church from within and without must prevail. As civilizations come and go, the worldwide Church continues to flourish, just not in our land. Since 1910 the Christian faith has grown by almost 2 billion people and is now a third of the world's populace.

In America, social and cultural habits provide stiff competition for one's faith or lack thereof. I think the shift began in the late 60's when narcissism became a well-known word and a heavily practiced form of worship, and has increased exponentially each year since. Our culture is saturated with instruction that the individual is preeminent in importance to just about anything else that lives. Sole care and concern for oneself to the exclusion of all human interaction with others in our family, organizations, churches. A plethora of data and just a simple observation of our culture will clearly demonstrate the slide of faith-based thought and practice. The scales and pendulum will one day swing and balance in the other direction much like it did after we abolished slavery. There are 45 million slaves in our world today; higher than at any time in the annals of Western Civilization. And, that figure does not include those in our own country who are slaves—to the treadmill of narcissism. Many believe that people of faith are weird, different, and oppressive. Those same people believe that church is all about structures, liturgy, repetition, monotony, and a plea for money to keep it all going. Andy Stanley, a Christian pastor stated that "A church is a gathering of people in process; a place where the curious, the unconvinced, the skeptical, the used-to-believe and the broken, as well as the committed, informed and sold out come together." Take a moment and watch a YouTube video of a song by Idina Menzel, "At This Table." The song presents in a very relevant manner the epitome of Christ's Church.

Whenever I have an opportunity to describe my idea of the Christian faith, my very simple answer is that it provides an enormous venue and vetting platform to make life better for a bazillion places in the world that are choked with strife. Over my life span, I have probably befriended well over a thousand people whom I know by name. None of them that I am aware of have all of their life puzzles completed. Almost all have been faced with cataclysmic events somewhere along the way. When all of the self-help books, magazine articles, clinics, prescription drugs and a litany of offered cures for the dreary, olive drab chunks of life have failed, you might find solace in a place filled with people who have similar lists of your life's woes, but who also have a heart and soul that yearns to help. If that simple response is not enough, then the Christian church is likely not suited to you. And, if you have read this far and are still looking for a reason to consider a faith connection, especially if you have adolescents or know people who do, find a church that has a rich and active youth program and figure out a way to have your kids pay a visit. I know of no other place; mental health wards, AA and NA, school counselors offices or any others you may know that have a better understanding of moral compasses and from where True North gets its bearing. A church youth program and para church organizations such as Young Life, Campus Crusade (Now Tru), Student Venture, Athletes in Action, and so many others have a grasp of orienteering for young people and are usually free. The word 'saved' might have new meaning for you.

Chapter Thirty-Three

"Why are there so many songs about rainbows
And what's on the other side?
Rainbows are vision, but only illusions
And rainbows have nothing to hide"
Jim Henson, Steve Whitmire
Rainbow Connection

I guess the point of all of this diatribe is a reflection on significant people along one's timeline, both good and bad, that so clearly define the path of one's life.

I remember the names of most of those wonderful people as well as those of the dark side. All are now likely gone, otherwise I would give them their due credit by naming them. One, in particular, was an English professor at CU, Kaye Bache-Snyder. She was my professor for the retake of first semester English Composition after failing the course on my first pass. Several weeks into the class, she called me aside and queried about why I was taking this course in the Spring. When I informed her that I failed it in the Fall, she expressed genuine concern about that. She shared with me that I was a very good writer and should consider writing as a major, or at least, a minor. Smoking marijuana was becoming the vogue on campus in the early 60's, and I thought that she had perhaps been toking a bit too much. Her simple expression of encouragement that day had an enormous impact on my self-esteem and self-worth. I had forgotten her name until reading her obit very recently. It was divine providence that I saw the notice of her passing as I was finishing my manuscript and I could acknowledge her skill as a prof. How simple a gesture, yet a direction changer for my self-esteem. But, all of us have those types of people throughout our lives. It is too bad that we can't somehow cull the wheat from the chaff with our life associations and avoid some agony.

I have mostly regretted the loss of my summers from the age of 7 through 21, but I know that the trials that I faced in the unusual episode of that part of my life, obviously gifted to me life skills that simply would not let me fail, or led me to believe that anything was achievable. None of my family has ever disdained the discipline of hard work and all have succeeded in life. It also provided a family cohesion that I don't see today in our fast paced, social media driven world.

If you are concerned about the never-summer mode of my life ever ending, I can assure you that the following years after college and beyond, I became a summer child. For many years during the summer months, I would always feel short changed if I wasn't outside doing something summery at least until dark. For almost 60 years my summers have been filled with everything I love to do. The playlist of my loves is long and would fill another book. Maybe later.

It may be just a coincidence that in a society where families are far flung around the globe, that all of my siblings, their children and my children and their children, for the most part, are geographically close by. I delight in family gatherings when we have 15 to 20 people seated around a harvest table when organized chaos is the norm. I think a harvest table surrounded by loved ones is a great metaphor for life and something sadly missing in the sociological experiment of modern-day-fractured-family structures and the social media phenomenon.

The best part of my life was finding my forever mate, after sifting through any number of 'perfect' matches that God was wise enough to steer me away from. She was blessed with the same unfailing family gene pool that believed in the rock solid traits of hard work, faith, education, agape love, believing that 'til death do us part' allows for no alternative but to make it work. My Suzi Creamcheese.

In retrospect, if the trials of my youthful years accomplished the formation of an inseparable bond with my family and established a hunger for the same for my progeny, I'll gladly not seek a mulligan for those years. My short stint in the military also led to similar relational connections that are still strong with those who still live.

As I look back on my life, I am blessed to know that my 'never summers' have produced 'never alone, and at least, a thousand rainbows.'

Epilogue

I recently had the privilege of reading the book, *Denison, Iowa* by Dale Maharidge. Maharidge wanted to do a story of a typical Midwestern town, how it began, the first settlers, the politics of the time and the comparisons of the town's character throughout its history. The book had a heavy emphasis on ethnic discrimination in the early years that never went away. Only the ethnicities had changed, but not the vitriol.

Maharidge pens a true story of a railroad boxcar getting mothballed on a railroad siding in Denison and abandoned for a number of months. A putrid odor from the boxcar eventually led to the discovery of 11 deceased immigrants from Mexico. Whoever was the last to die had arranged all of the bodies in a ceremonious-like line, shoulder to shoulder and added his own body to the end of the line before he too succumbed.

The book has numerous anecdotal stories of the discrimination against the ethic people who have migrated to Dension to work in meat and pork packing plants, doing those menial, nasty jobs that the locals will no longer do. The malevolence between the current ethnic groups clearly mirroring the stories in the book of the early Germans being hated by the

Scandinavians and trying to burn each other's properties.

After spending 13 summers of my life doing some of the menial work almost totally performed now by Latinos, I have a much greater perspective on the intricacies of trying to make the enormous melting pot that is the United States of America work as well as it does.

Writing 'Never Summer' has provoked a great interest in the astounding contrasts of adolescent years over the span of three generations, both as an adolescent and my own youthful challenges, and having raised three striplings and watching them prepare for and live through their juvenile years, now nurturing their own. I can't imagine anyone presenting a contrary suggestion that those child rearing efforts are better or in any way easier today.

About the Author

Stan Nicholas is an octogenarian who is writing about unusual personal life stories that span almost three generations, with reflections on the issues of the myriad adolescent challenges that have so radically evolved from his own puerile experiences. He is married and has three married daughters and seven grandchildren, all in their formative years that have provided a stunning panorama of the complexities that generationZers endure and the radical escalation of trauma that face today's youth and their families' frantic attempts to understand and mitigate. It is through that scope that he is able to sift through the evolution of changing times within a family.